CHINESE CERAMI

HIGHLIGHTS OF THE SIR PERCIVAL DAVID COLLECTION

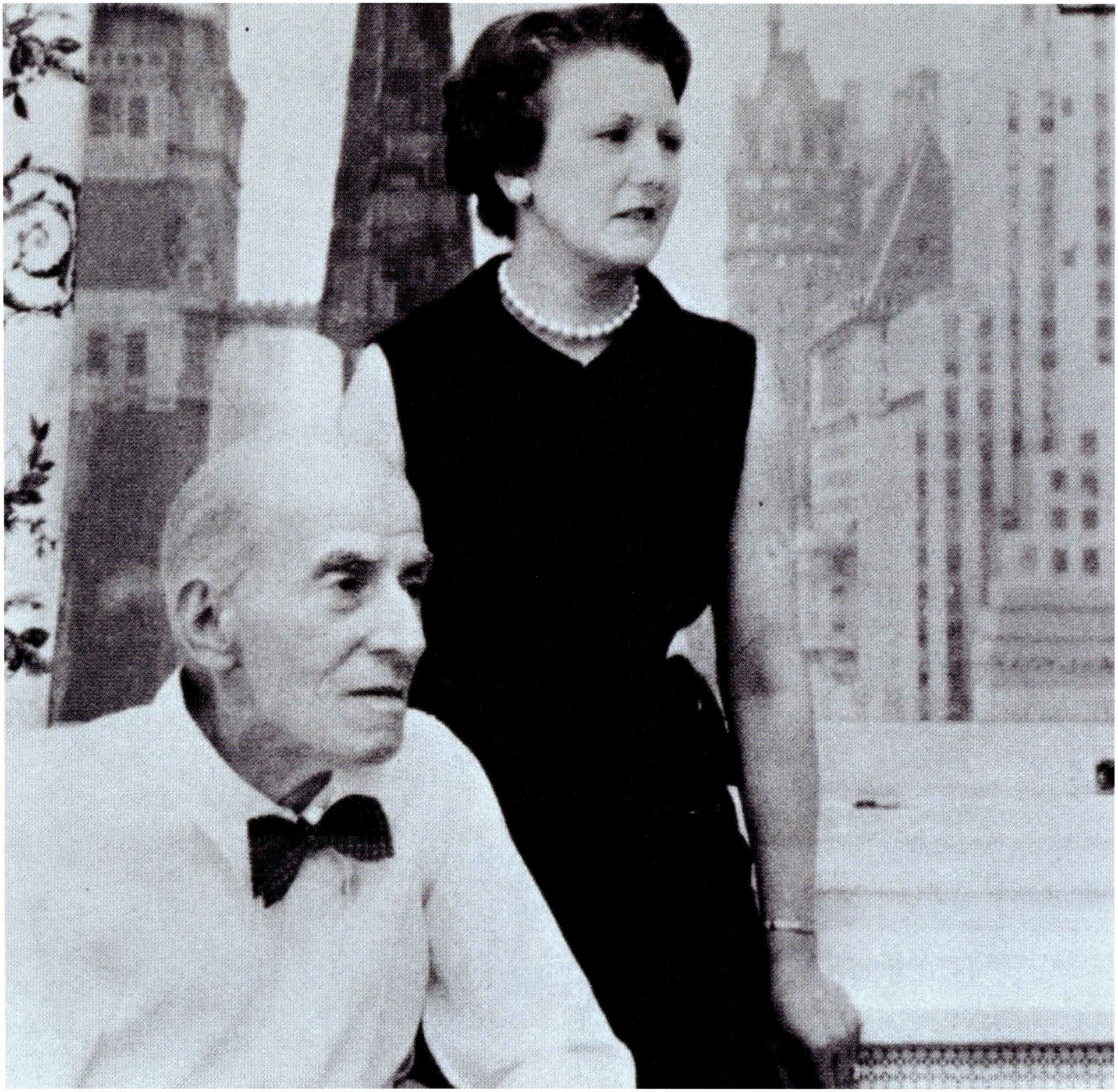

Sir Percival and Lady David in New York City in 1950 (photo courtesy Suzanne G. Valenstein and SOAS)

CHINESE CERAMICS

HIGHLIGHTS OF THE SIR PERCIVAL DAVID COLLECTION

REGINA KRAHL AND JESSICA HARRISON-HALL

THE BRITISH MUSEUM PRESS

First published in 2009 by The British Museum Press
A division of The British Museum Company Ltd
38 Russell Square, London WC1B 3QQ
www.britishmuseum.org

Reprinted 2010

A catalogue record for this book is available from the British Library

ISBN 978-0-7141-2454-4

Photography by the British Museum Department of Photography and Imaging
(page 94, numbers 36, 39, 41: © SOAS. All rights reserved)

Designed and typeset in Dante by Peter Ward
Printed in Italy by Printer Trento

Contents

Director's Foreword

The opening of a new gallery to display the world-famous Sir Percival David Collection of Chinese art at the British Museum is a momentous event. Impressively large with almost 1700 ceramics and one painting, the Collection holds an extraordinary concentration of magnificent, in many cases imperial-quality, objects, the majority dating from the tenth to eighteenth centuries. Its special significance lies in the exceedingly rich assemblage of marked and inscribed ceramics that offer critical evidence about dating and manufacture, and also provide commentaries from admiring connoisseurs such as the Qianlong emperor (ruled 1736–95). Sir Percival David's (1892–1964) unusual, indeed invaluable, focus on ceramics with inscriptions reflects his scholarly predilections. His belief in the power of education led him to present the University of London with his Collection, which opened to the public in 1952 in a nineteenth-century Bloomsbury townhouse.

At the turn of the twenty-first century, with the townhouse requiring major renovation, continued display of the Collection presented a major challenge. Upon learning that the University and the Percival David Foundation were seeking a new venue, Sir Joseph Hotung was inspired to suggest the British Museum, where millions of viewers every year will have easy access to the Collection. It is now displayed in its entirety here in a custom-designed gallery adjoined by a Study Centre located within the Sir Joseph Hotung Centre for Ceramic Studies. The new setting resonates with David's hope that his collection would be well exhibited and closely studied. Through Sir Joseph Hotung's generous sponsorship, the Museum is delighted to be able to honour and expand Sir Percival David's wish and to share his Collection widely. The recently opened gallery, this book and the Collection's presentation on the Museum's website allow the entire world to celebrate its outstanding quality.

Developments for the transfer of the Collection occurred at a rapid pace and too many individuals to name have greatly exerted themselves on behalf of this project. I should, however, like to specially thank the Protection Nominees of the Percival David Foundation, John Franks and Colin Sheaf, for the loan of the Collection which is renewable in perpetuity. I am also grateful to senior faculty at the University of London and the School for Oriental and African Studies for their co-operation and collegiality. The contributions of our outside academic advisor, Regina Krahl, and my colleagues within the Museum have been invaluable. The unveiling of the Sir Percival David Collection in its new home, in the context of a world ceramic collection, will, we hope, ensure that those who are passionate about China (and china) will now find the British Museum an ever richer store of knowledge and delight.

Neil MacGregor
Director of the British Museum

Keeper's Foreword and Acknowledgements

The Sir Joseph Hotung Centre for Ceramic Studies is a fabulous new asset for the British Museum. Its heart is devoted to the display of the Sir Percival David Collection in a complete redesign of the space formerly the Music Library, which relocated a decade ago to the new British Library. Experienced synaesthetically, the new ceramic gallery still pulsates with rhythm, melody and harmony, the visual music coming alive through the relationships of glaze colours, painted decoration and potted forms. Two hundred exceptional ceramics featured in centre cases present major highlights of the Chinese ceramic tradition, while the remainder fill wall cases, library-style, on floor-to-ceiling shelves. Stellar examples in each bay serve as a focus to elucidate the groupings.

In 1925 Sir Percival David was invited by the Chinese to consult on plans to display ceramics at the new Palace Museum in Beijing. This rare opportunity to handle the imperial collection set him apart from his fellow Western enthusiasts, informing his collecting and connoisseurship and leading him to build a collection unparalleled for its combination of scholarly interest and dazzling beauty. At the British Museum, these ceramics will continue to inspire visitors the way Sir Percival and Lady David had always intended, but in far greater numbers than before.

Also in accord with Sir Percival's wishes, the collection will remain a centre for academic enquiry. Evidence from recent excavations and studies has been brought to bear on the evaluation of the ceramics in this publication. The former curators of the collection, Lady David, Margaret Medley, Rosemary Scott and Stacey Pierson, raised a high bar for standards of scholarship, and their work on the collection is gratefully acknowledged.

Sir Joseph Hotung's vision and generosity in bringing the collection to the British Museum is deeply appreciated and will resonate positively long into the future. It has been wonderful to work with the Percival David Foundation Trustees, John Franks and Colin Sheaf, and much thanks is due for their support.

A project of this complexity relies upon the skills and teamwork of many, but here only a few can be named. Outside the Museum, Regina Krahl served as valued academic advisor and consulting curator. Luisa Mengoni on short-term contract skilfully kicked off plans as co-ordinating curator. The gallery design and graphics reflect the gifted vision of Karl Abeyasekera, Bill Kerridge and Mash Chudasama, who worked closely with Geoffrey Pickup of the British Museum.

In house, Carol Michaelson's advocacy for the project and advice have been invaluable from the start. Jessica Harrison-Hall has been a guiding light at every point in her role as the lead curator, and her expertise, intelligence and efficiency are reflected throughout. Mike Davis served as project manager par excellence, orchestrating every detail of the build and keeping the project on schedule with good humour. Steve Slack skilfully directed interpretation and Katherine Brooks led on the care of objects, including packing and installation. Loretta Hogan managed an extraordinary programme of ceramics conservation. Dudley Hubbard, photographer, and Nina Shandloff, editor, have ensured the high quality of this book to celebrate the new gallery.

Finally, the deepest appreciation is owed to Sir Percival David, whose knowledge and passion for Chinese ceramics created a legacy that profoundly touches the lives of all of us interested in Chinese culture.

Jan Stuart
Keeper of Asia Department, British Museum

The Sir Percival David Collection of Chinese Ceramics

The Sir Percival David Collection of Chinese Ceramics is one of the world's finest, and Sir Percival (1892–1964) was a remarkable man. Little is known about his personal or professional life; his passion was collecting and for him this was not a dilettante leisure occupation. In the tradition of China's literati connoisseurs, he strove to understand the geographical and historical background of the objects he admired, and their appreciation in past centuries. This required knowledge and research, command of the Chinese language, visits to China and the reading of historical texts. Sir Percival started young, aged twenty-two, and within four decades had assembled the most significant private collection of Chinese ceramics.

The decades around the collapse of the Qing dynasty (AD 1644–1911) were a fruitful period for collectors of Chinese art. Family heirlooms came on the market, and sales from the Imperial Palace were not uncommon. Objects from the Forbidden City were used as collateral against bank loans, or sold, more or less openly, by the *neiwufu* [内務府], the erstwhile Imperial Household Department, which continued to look after the former imperial family, its staff and its palaces, or by anyone with access to court holdings.[1] Unfortunately, the acquisition history of Sir Percival's collection is unrecorded: almost no piece can be directly traced to the imperial collection, although many are likely to have originated there.[2]

Perhaps Sir Percival's most important collecting achievement is to have reunited a pair of vases that are the cornerstone for dating China's earliest blue-and-white porcelain and became associated with his name, the David Vases (no. 24). One came from Mountstuart Elphinstone in the 1920s, the other he purchased at auction in 1935 from the Charles E. Russell collection.[3] Elphinstone is also the source of a group of mostly monochrome porcelains that he donated to the newly established Percival David Foundation before it opened to the public in 1952. Until then, Sir Percival's collection had been anything but static: items came and went, and he made numerous donations to both the Victoria and Albert and the British Museum.

Sir Percival's selection was dictated less by taste than with a view towards education. At a time when Chinese ceramics were still largely bought for decoration, he was looking for quality of workmanship and historical importance. He was not the only discerning collector of the time interested in Song (AD 960–1279) and earlier wares – they had already been discovered by a small group of collectors who in 1921 had founded the Oriental Ceramic Society in England; but he recognized earlier than most of his peers the quality of imperial wares from the Ming (AD 1368–1644) and Qing (AD 1644–1911) dynasties. He also realized the historical importance of documentary inscriptions and treasured imperial provenance, as conveyed by poems engraved by the Qianlong emperor (ruled AD 1736–95), China's greatest imperial collector.

Sir Percival did not aim to cover the complete history of Chinese ceramics. The collection does not include any examples of the soft, permeable earthenwares which technically are not very different from pottery made in other parts of the world. He concentrated on the hard and dense stonewares and porcelains, upon which China's fame as a ceramic-producing country is based. The collection is often called the most important collection of imperial wares outside China, but it is more than that. It gives a representative overview of the development of ceramics unique to China.

In the 1930s he considered the collection ready for publication and commissioned the foremost ceramic scholar of the day, R.L. Hobson, to compile a catalogue.[4]

In 1931 he had already established a chair of Chinese Art and Archaeology at the University of London and in 1950 he donated the collection to the University. A townhouse in Gordon Square, intended as temporary lodgings, provided exhibition space from 1952 until 2007 and received generations of students and ceramic devotees. In its new home in the Sir Joseph Hotung Centre for Ceramic Studies in the British Museum it finally has a purpose-built gallery with an adjacent study room.

Through his patronage and his own research Sir Percival made major contributions to scholarship, and scholarship since then has made great leaps forward. Nationwide archaeological exploration in China, systematic excavation reports, the opening and publication of former imperial holdings, and the scrutiny of more and more historical texts have brought on a veritable avalanche of new evidence in recent decades. This has led to some changes in attribution during the review of the collection for its new display and to some surprise finds, a few of which will be introduced below.

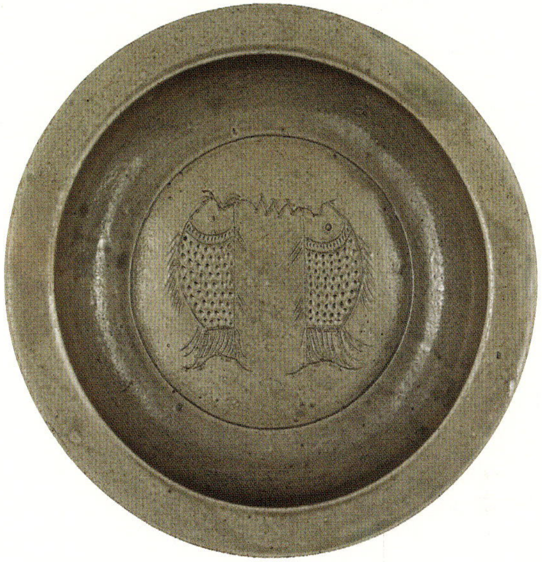

Fig. 1 (PDF 250)
Green-glazed stoneware basin incised with twin fish
Shaoxing, northern Zhejiang province
Western Jin dynasty, 3rd century AD
Diameter 33.6 cm

Early Ceramics

Chinese potters made a pioneering discovery in ceramic technology in the Bronze Age, in the late second millennium BC. In kilns of the southeastern region of Zhejiang/Jiangsu, at firing temperatures above 1200°C ceramics vitrified, that is, they became hard, dense, resistant, durable, clean and thus highly practical. Wood ash floating through the kiln provided a natural glaze which would soon be applied deliberately. The physical qualities of these stonewares and the aesthetic attraction of their shiny olive-green glazes were features until then known only from precious materials. In the West comparable wares were not made until the fifteenth century AD. From south of the Yangzi they even reached the faraway centres of power in the north near the Yellow River; although such a great distance must have thwarted their wider dissemination.

As elsewhere in the world, China's main ceramic product until the Tang dynasty (AD 618–907) was earthenware pottery, a relatively soft and porous material fired at below 1100°C. If in the Neolithic period (from about the seventh millennium BC) it had been the prime material for receptacles, the introduction of bronze in the Shang period (*c.* 1600–*c.* 1050 BC) turned it into a cheaper alternative, used for lesser items of daily life and to replace more precious wares for burial in graves. No such items are in Sir Percival's collection.

In the Six Dynasties period (AD 222–589), with the Chinese capital at Nanjing in Jiangsu and the north under foreign control, southern ceramic manufacture received a boost. The production in northern Zhejiang of glazed stonewares, consistent in quality, with yellowish-green or occasionally black glazes and decorated in a variety of techniques, became a large-scale industry. This is when Sir Percival's collection begins (fig. 1). Although a poem of the third century AD mentions a wine vessel of such green stoneware, the ware's main use was for burial.[5] Ewers with spouts not pierced or too narrow for pouring, plates with cups and spoons affixed, or basins with ring handles applied as pure decoration were not conceived as functional objects.

The north of China lagged behind in its development of ceramics. Due to different geological formations of the northern and southern parts of the Chinese landmass, the loessic wheat- and millet-growing regions of the north and the quartz-rich rice-growing lands of the south provided potters with different raw materials and fuels and generated differences in kiln technology.[6] With the divide between the two regions falling between the Yellow and Yangzi Rivers, most of Shandong, Henan, Shaanxi and Gansu belonged to the northern sphere, and most of Jiangsu, Anhui, Hubei and Sichuan to the southern.

Ruled by nomadic tribes under the dynastic name Wei (AD 386–557), the north experienced a period of warfare and unrest, but also an extraordinary movement of peoples and an influx of foreign goods and ideas from Western Asia. This sense of a new era about to dawn perhaps led to a new departure in ceramics as well. By the Northern Qi period (AD 550–77) several kilns had emerged in Hebei and Henan which made fine stonewares, not only in green and black as in the south, but also in white. These soon included pure white and translucent pieces fired to about 1300°C – the world's first porcelains. This heralded a thousand years' monopoly and made China's name synonymous with porcelain.[7]

By the Tang period ceramics – mainly stonewares – had become items of value. They formed part of lavish imperial donations to a revered Buddhist relic near the capital,[8] and whole shiploads were sailed westwards,

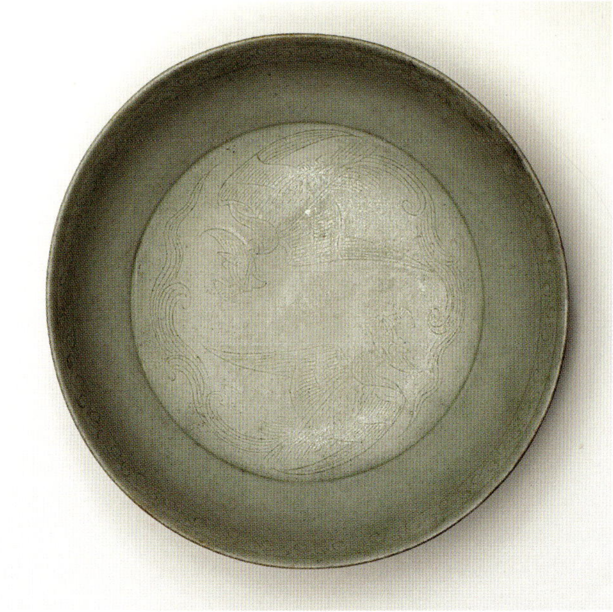

Fig. 2 (PDF 262)
Yue ware dish with a pair of phoenix, the character *yong* ['eternal'] engraved on the base
Yue kilns, Shanglinhu, northern Zhejiang province
Tang dynasty, late 9th or early 10th century AD
Diameter 17.5 cm

where local potters made imitations.[9] Inland, connoisseurship developed with the cult of tea drinking, which required carefully selected utensils. Manufacturing centres became known by name. Yue wares with glazes evoking green jade came from Yuezhou, the region around Shanglinhu in northern Zhejiang (fig. 2), which had the longest stoneware tradition. Copies, though not very close, appeared in the north, at the Yaozhou kilns of Huangpuzhen near Tongchuan in Shaanxi. Xing wares of a sparkling white reminiscent of silver were made at Neiqiu and Lincheng in the region of Xingzhou in southern Hebei (no. 1); but Ding wares of Quyang in nearby Dingzhou can look so similar that the two are not always easy to tell apart (e.g. no. 2). For centuries green wares remained associated with the south, white wares with the north.

Song Dynasty Stonewares

In the Song period (AD 960–1279) fine ceramics were made all over China and had become fixtures of daily life. The ideological connotations of luxury items made of non-precious material perfectly suited the spirit of the time, when understatement was considered the utmost sophistication in taste. Of the hundreds, perhaps thousands, of kilns that were active, a dozen or so became famous for one trademark style. Such iconic wares inspired imitations, sometimes so close that in the Song precise identification of a kiln is not always possible and famous names designate a style rather than an actual place of origin.

In spite of this complexity the basic picture of Song ceramic manufacture is relatively simple, as the many types all derived from the basic Tang wares: white, green and black. Whereas in the Tang dynasty wood had been the prime fuel in kilns all over China, in the Song northern Chinese kilns switched to coal, while wood was still used in the south. Since the firing atmosphere in coal-burning kilns is mostly oxidizing, warmer, yellowish glaze tones predominate in the north, while wood-burning kilns facilitate reduction (of oxygen), which resulted in cooler, bluish tones in the south.

In the Northern Song period (AD 960–1127), with China's capital located at Kaifeng in Henan, the kilns of the north were the leading manufacturers; in the Southern Song (AD 1127–1279), after the court's move to Hangzhou in Zhejiang, the southern ones flourished. Northern production continued, however, without major disruption or loss of quality under the Jurchen conquerors, who called their dynasty Jin (AD 1115–1234).

The Ding and the Yaozhou kilns, secondary manufacturers during the Tang, both eclipsed their erstwhile models, Xing and Yue, and developed their own distinct style around the Five Dynasties period (AD 907–60). Their replacement of wood with coal as fuel provided Ding whites with a characteristic creamy colour reminiscent of ivory, and Yaozhou celadons with an olive-green glaze which emphasized all incised or impressed decoration. Their popularity, however, was very different: although their vessels were similar in quality and style, Yaozhou was rarely mentioned in the connoisseurs' literature and little represented in the imperial collection. Sir Percival, too, acquired only a very small group, but within it one of the finest extant examples (no. 9).

Ding, on the other hand, was one of the celebrated wares of the Song. Thinly potted, tactile, elegant, precious-looking and sometimes decorated with gold, Ding vessels represented the finest tablewares. Some inscriptions suggest use at court, such as 官 [*guan*, 'official'], 新官 [*xin guan*, 'new official'], 尚藥局 [*shangyao-ju*, 'Palace Medical Service'] or 尚食局 [*shangshiju*, 'Palace Food Service']. The small dish in the form of an arrowhead leaf (no. 2) bears an otherwise unrecorded inscription, 會稽 [*kuaiji*], previously interpreted as a place name, but in fact referring to the Palace Accounts Office.[10] Sir Percival's collection is extremely rich in high-quality Ding wares, including some very rare upright shapes (no. 8) and large basins decorated inside and out (no. 7).

For the court a more exclusive ware was fashioned for a brief period at the end of the Northern Song, from AD 1086 to 1106 or 1125. At first glance, the seeming simplicity of the celebrated Ru ware from Qingliangsi, Baofeng in Henan, formerly Ruzhou, may be disappointing. Ru is not a ware to impress when displayed, but one to seduce when handled. Generally of small size, Ru vessels are finely potted, usually undecorated and fully covered with a jewel-like blue-green glaze veined with a luminous crackle, as if made entirely of some precious stone. To achieve this effect vessels were fired standing on tiny supports that left unobtrusive 'sesame seed' markings.

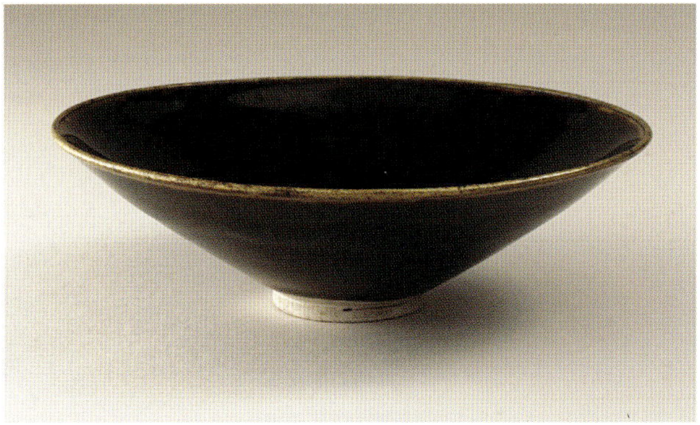

Fig. 3 (PDF 300)
Black-glazed Ding bowl
Ding kilns, Quyang, Hebei province
Northern Song dynasty, 11th or 12th century AD
Diameter 18.5 cm

In spite of being the most desirable of all Song wares Ru was little copied, probably because of a dearth of models to imitate. Sir Percival assembled the largest collection of intact Ru pieces (as opposed to fragments and wasters excavated at the kiln site) outside the National Palace Museum, Taipei. It includes remarkable examples with incised decoration (no. 4), an exceedingly rare vase (no. 5), and one of the largest vessels in existence (no. 6). A stand like no. 3 is depicted in an eighteenth-century court painting in a palace interior supporting a blue porcelain bowl.[11]

Black wares, whether northern or southern, never enjoyed a reputation comparable to green and white wares. Like other coarser ceramics, such as the Cizhou wares of Guantai in Hebei province, they were made from relatively rough, dark clays and therefore considered as rustic utilitarian ceramics typically used for storage, rather than elegant tablewares. No northern black-ware kiln managed to make a name for itself, and in the south only two kiln centres became known for their tea bowls: the Jian kilns of Jianyang in Fujian and the Jizhou kilns of Ji'an in Jiangxi. Like China's traditional connoisseurs, Sir Percival largely ignored black wares, although he did acquire one stunning black tea bowl, a rather uncharacteristic product of the Ding kilns (fig. 3).

A much more popular ware, Jun, also derived from Tang black wares. Milky-blue splashes on black glazes provoked by wood-ash deposits were developed at the Juntai kilns in Yu county, Henan province, into striking opal-blue glazes (no. 10). Even more flamboyant effects – unique among Song wares – were achieved by combining this with copper to create bright purple hues (no. 11) or splashes (no. 12).

Besides these simple wheel-made pieces, there exists another very different type of Jun ware: mould-made flower vessels glazed in blue or purple with incised numerals from 1 to 10 on the base, possibly to associate flowerpots with stands (no. 21). This group, which for decades had been attributed to the Northern Song period on account of reputed archaeological evidence, is today widely believed to represent imperial flower vessels of the early Ming,[12] perhaps commissioned to furnish the newly built palaces of the Forbidden City in the Yongle reign (AD 1403–24). Jun ware of both types is richly represented in Sir Percival's collection.

When the Song court, after repeated attacks by nomadic tribes from the north, was forced to abandon its capital and move south in AD 1127, it lost access to its traditional ceramic suppliers. Installed at the 'temporary seat' in Hangzhou, Zhejiang province, which remained the capital throughout the Southern Song period, the Gaozong emperor (ruled AD 1127–62) had an official kiln established there under the auspices of the Palace Maintenance Office [修内司, *xiuneisi*]. Although modelled on Ru ware, this new southern *guan* [官, 'official'] ware had its own character, with richer and thicker glazes in mysterious bluish and greyish tones (no. 15), usually with a prominent crackle as its only decorative feature. The best glazes and crackle 'patterns', which can resemble cracked ice, were never achieved elsewhere (nos 13, 14, 16),

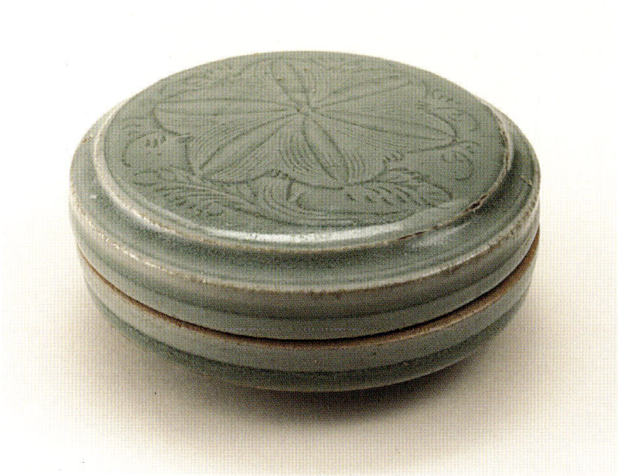

Fig. 4 (PDF 282)
Longquan celadon cosmetics or seal paste box with a morning glory
Longquan kilns, southern Zhejiang province
Five Dynasties or Northern Song, 10th or 11th century AD
Diameter 8.2 cm

although *guan* ware was massively copied at all times (fig. 7). Song *guan* ware, but not the most exquisite types, has been excavated at the Laohudong kiln site in Hangzhou.

A small metropolitan enterprise of this kind was ideal for a high-quality output but on a small scale. Mass production was possible in vast kiln centres in rural southern China: those of Longquan in Zhejiang made green celadon wares, and those of Raozhou, modern Jingdezhen in Jiangxi, specialized in white, so-called *qingbai* [青白] wares (*qing* referring to a bluish-green tone; *bai* meaning white). If the Longquan kilns' early production was still influenced by Yue ware (fig. 4), they developed their own style in the Southern Song. Simple and well-proportioned shapes were covered with rich layers of smooth blue-green glazes, with minimal or no decoration (nos 17, 18). The best pieces come close to *guan* ware and were greatly valued, but much of the large output was destined for export. Some five hundred 'dragon' kilns of gigantic scale have been located in the Longquan region, and these could reach a hundred metres in length and accommodate tens of thousands of pieces.

The contemporary white wares of Jingdezhen, thinly potted, highly translucent and with an attractive touch of blue, were comparatively little esteemed in the Song. Their heyday was to come in the Yuan. The different traditional evaluation of these two wares is reflected in Sir Percival's collection, where Longquan celadon is plentiful and *qingbai* scarce.

Yuan Dynasty Porcelains

As the Mongols conquered and reunited China under the dynastic name Yuan (AD 1279–1368), a revolution of taste took place in the art world. The understated elegance cultivated by the Song court and its scholar-officials went out of fashion. The new rulers, however, dictated no particular taste, and official wares were rather modest. As the colour white was revered, Jingdezhen's fine white porcelains were an obvious choice. Some are inscribed 樞府 [*shufu*], referring to the Bureau of Military Affairs, and a unique dish decorated with phoenixes, emblem of the empress, bears the reign name of Aragibag (Alajiba), an infant heir to the throne who 'ruled' for only two months in AD 1328 (fig. 5). Since loyalists still fought for his line four years after rival factions had taken over, it may slightly postdate this period.

Without an imperial model to follow, taste was shaped by more popular forces, including a large and influential foreign population which demanded more down-to-earth styles, more colour, more decoration, more drama altogether. Plain vessels, such as the exquisite ewer (no. 19) with a minimalist silhouette, as if its profile were designed on the drawing board, are the exception. More typical are carved, moulded, stamped, applied and openwork decoration, and attempts to add colour. The

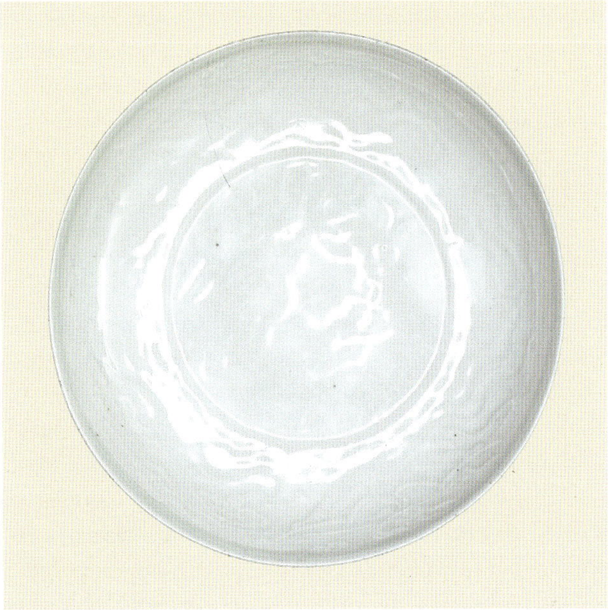

Fig. 5 (PDF A409)
White-glazed stoneware dish with moulded phoenix, inscribed 天順年造 [*Tianshun nian zao*, 'made in the Tianshun period', i.e. AD 1328]
Jingdezhen kilns, Jiangxi province
Yuan dynasty, AD 1328–32
Diameter 21 cm

green Longquan glazes were enlivened with iron-brown spots (no. 20) or unglazed designs that fired a contrasting reddish brown. The white Jingdezhen wares were painted or glazed in cobalt blue (no. 22), copper red or iron brown – pigments suitable for the high firing temperatures of porcelain; yet pieces as elaborate as no. 23 with complex applied motifs in two colours remained rarities.

The style that conquered the world was blue-and-white. In the early fourteenth century the Jingdezhen kilns quickly mastered a bold painting manner in a vivid cobalt blue, applied under the glaze and therefore permanent. In Chinese connoisseurs' circles this new style with its dense and powerful aspect in a bright, imported colour was not immediately accepted, but abroad it was soon universally copied and left a lasting impression on ceramics world-wide. For the new clientele new shapes were developed in unprecedented sizes. A unique pair of vases, made for a temple near Jingdezhen in AD 1351 together with a censer (now lost) and inscribed to that effect, provides the only precise evidence for the dating of Yuan blue-and-white (no. 24). These 'David Vases' show a wonderful cross section through the period's decorative repertoire.

Ming Dynasty Porcelains

In the Ming (AD 1368–1644) access to fine porcelain became an imperial privilege. Virtually all Chinese porcelain came from Jingdezhen, whose kilns were supervised by the court; their output was submitted to strict quality control and any rejects destroyed and buried. The xenophobic Hongwu emperor (ruled AD 1368–98) closed up a country that had been an open, international trading place during Mongol rule. The loss of foreign customers and a lack of imported cobalt temporarily created a somewhat insipid, formal style, in dramatic contrast to the exuberant, lively mode of the Yuan. Cobalt fired a pale blue, or was replaced by copper (a notoriously difficult pigment to master) for red designs. Sir Percival acquired one of the rare successfully fired examples (no. 25).

The reigns of Yongle (AD 1403–24) and Xuande (AD 1426–35), on the other hand, were a golden age for Jingdezhen, and here Sir Percival's collection is at its strongest. Yongle blue-and-white shows Middle Eastern shapes and styles (nos 26, 27) as well as designs inspired by Chinese ink painting (no. 28). As the Yongle emperor embarked on massive maritime expeditions to the West, much porcelain was officially traded abroad. Only from the Xuande period was blue-and-white specifically conceived for the court, which meant smaller formats and more concise decoration (compare nos 29 and 30). This is

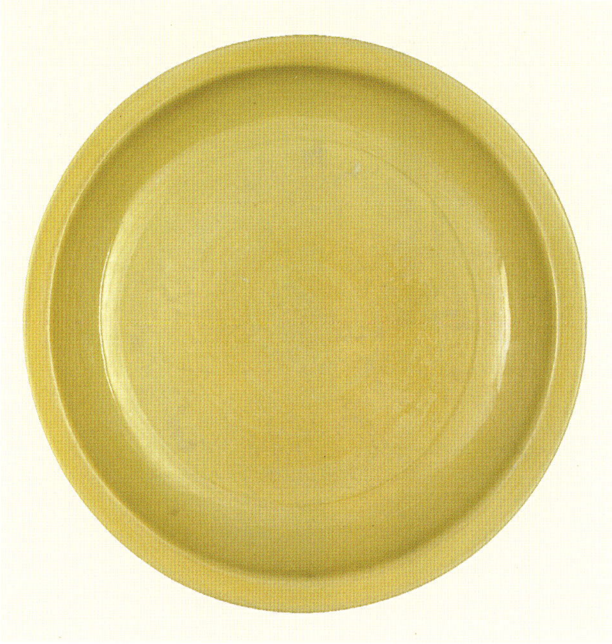

Fig. 6 (PDF 582)
Yellow-glazed porcelain dish with flat rim and gilt bands
Jingdezhen kilns, Jiangxi province
Ming dynasty, Yongle period, AD 1403–24
Diameter 31.6 cm

the period when imperial reign marks were introduced, probably following the Yongle custom of imperial dedications on Buddhist bronzes.

This imperial attention prompted great activity at the kilns. The exploration of their waste heaps in recent decades has revealed that unprecedented experiments took place with a multitude of colours and ways to employ them, so much so that after the Xuande period no real further innovation was made until the Kangxi reign (AD 1662–1722). Experiments deemed unsuccessful never saw the light of day; others survived in rare examples. The most exciting new discovery in Sir Percival's collection is two yellow-glazed dishes of the Yongle period – a type of which otherwise only sherds appear to have survived in Jingdezhen. One with a flat rim and an unglazed white base bears traces of gilt decoration as known from rare Yongle white wares (fig. 6); the other, with a flared rim (and perhaps fractionally later), reveals the characteristic reddish fired biscuit under a thin transparent glaze at the base (no. 31). Both are exceptional in quality, with a silky surface and vivid colour, superior to any other yellow piece in the collection.

Copper-red glazes were successfully fired only in the Yongle and Xuande reigns and virtually discontinued thereafter due to technical difficulties (no. 32). In the Xuande period a bright turquoise enamel was introduced (no. 33), and cobalt was used both for an even, high-fired and a rare mottled, low-fired blue glaze known as 'snowflake blue' (no. 34). Polychrome effects were achieved by combining cobalt blue with underglaze copper red (no. 30 left), overglaze iron red (no. 30 right), or yellow enamel (no. 35), and rarely also using several enamels.

After a so-called interregnum (AD 1436–64) of three short reigns that did not produce any imperial porcelain, the Chenghua emperor (ruled AD 1465–87) revived imperial patronage but on a reduced scale. Chenghua porcelains, usually small in size and tranquil in style, have an unrivalled tactile quality (fig. 7). Painted designs have an intimate character far from machine-like perfection. The most distinctive style is known as *doucai* [鬥彩], a term describing the interaction between underglaze-blue outlines and overglaze yellow, red, green and aubergine washes, which has been variously translated as 'interlocking', 'dove-tailed', 'contending', 'contrasting', 'joined colours', etc. (no. 38). *Doucai* chicken cups (no. 37) and grape stem cups with their charming naturalistic designs became trophy collectors' pieces avidly sought after even by later emperors. To find seven Chenghua 'palace bowls', which come in only about a dozen patterns (no. 36), and eight Chenghua *doucai* pieces in one collection is sensational.

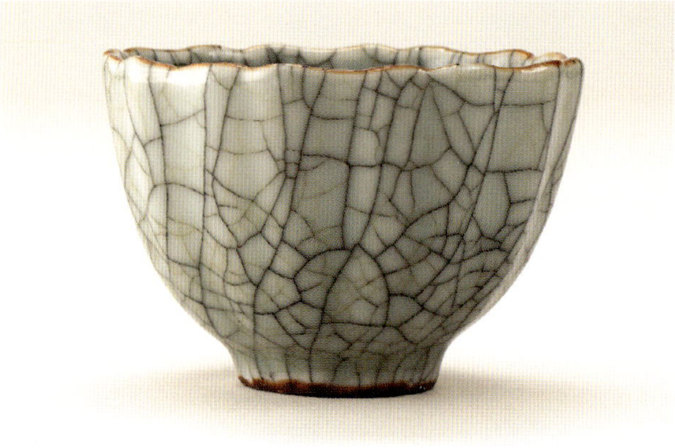

Fig. 7 (PDF A57)
Flower-shaped porcelain cup with grey-green crackled glaze
Jingdezhen kilns, Jiangxi province
Ming dynasty, Chenghua mark and period, AD 1465–87
Diameter 9.1 cm

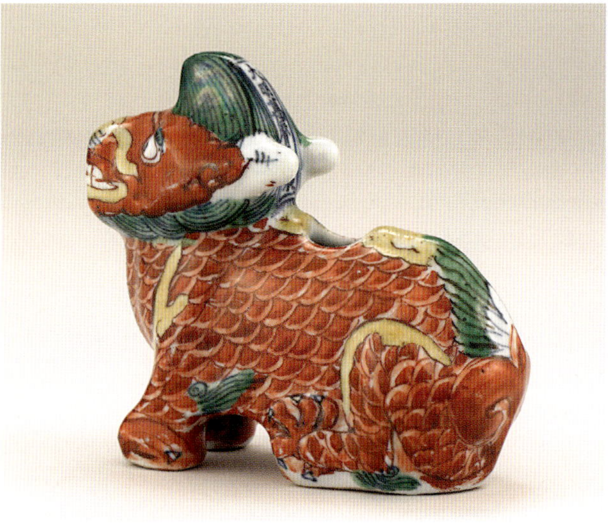

Fig. 8 (PDF A713)
Polychrome painted [五彩, *wucai*] porcelain figure of a fabulous animal [麒麟, *qilin*]
Jingdezhen kilns, Jiangxi province
Ming dynasty, Wanli mark and period, AD 1573–1620
Length 10.8 cm

The later Ming reigns – Hongzhi, Zhengde, Jiajing, Longqing and Wanli (AD 1488–1620) – were less inventive and are dominated by variation rather than innovation (no. 39). Some peculiar pieces with Persian Islamic or Portuguese Christian inscriptions date from the Zhengde period (AD 1506–21); some of them are even inscribed with the imperial reign mark. In subsequent reigns conventional colours were used in new combinations (no. 40), and with underglaze blue employed for washes rather than outlines the former *doucai* style became *wucai* [五彩, 'five colours'] (fig. 8). After Wanli, the imperial kilns stopped working and did not start again until the Kangxi period of the next dynasty, the Qing.

Qing Dynasty Porcelains

The Qing dynasty (AD 1644–1911) was a period of unprecedented imperial patronage of porcelain in which quality was catapulted to the highest levels ever achieved. Porcelain production received the personal attention of three rulers, whose interests differed. Technical challenges fascinated the Kangxi emperor (ruled AD 1662–1722) (nos 41, 45), aesthetic refinement the Yongzheng emperor (ruled AD 1723–35) (nos 42, 43, 44, 47), and an exhaustive display of his artisans' talents the Qianlong emperor (ruled AD 1736–95) (no. 50 and figs 9, 10).

The Kangxi emperor established imperial workshops inside the Forbidden City, in close proximity to the emperors' living quarters, where they could observe, applaud and criticize the works from nearby. Porcelain could not be made there because of the noise and dirt this involved, but blanks supplied from Jingdezhen could be decorated there and the enamels fired on in small kilns at lower temperatures. Western Jesuits, who brought to the court artistic know-how together with raw materials, had introduced new enamel colours, which were here applied to copper, porcelain and glass. Even long after the enamels were locally produced, this Beijing

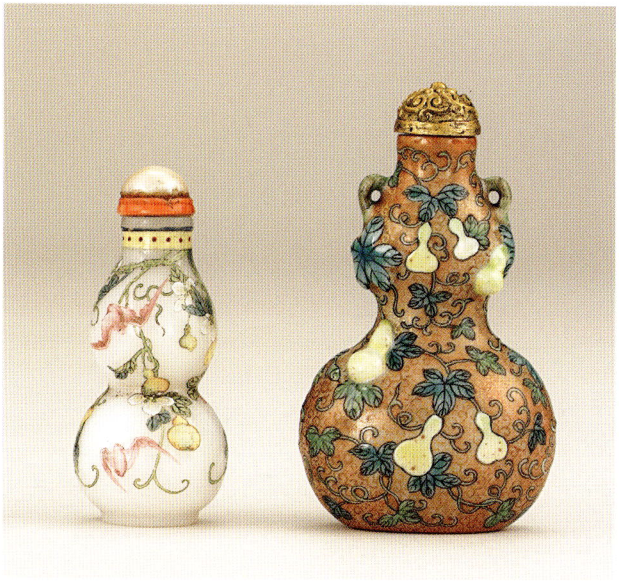

Fig. 9 (PDF 813 and 836)
Gourd-shaped snuff bottles of painted glass and painted porcelain, with coral-and-pearl and gilt-bronze stoppers, respectively
Beijing Palace Workshops, and Jingdezhen kilns, Jiangxi province, respectively
Qing dynasty, Qianlong marks and period, AD 1736–95
Heights 4.7 cm and 5.5 cm

enamel work was still called *falangcai* [珐瑯彩, 'foreign colours'].

The first porcelains painted in the Forbidden City showed formalized flower designs on fully enamelled grounds following models on copper (no. 45). In this experimental phase the range of shades was particularly wide, as colours had not yet been standardized. New enamels introduced from the West were a rose pink which dominated the traditional palette from then on and an opaque white of even greater impact as, mixed with other enamels, it opened the way to a whole new range of shades and pastel tones.

The Yongzheng reign saw the creation of painterly masterpieces. Ink painting had already inspired porcelain painters in the Yongle reign but their technical means were limited (see no. 28). With the extensive new palette, paintings on porcelain could now be achieved which, accompanied by colophons and mock seals, resembled very closely paintings on silk. Restricting colouration deliberately to that of monochrome ink and seal paste, as on the superb pair of bowls (no. 47), was the ultimate step towards a complete transfer of ink painting to porcelain.

In the Qianlong period decoration became more complex and labour-intensive. Tiny details, such as the webbed feet of geese on no. 48, were rendered with several different enamels; and the European-style painting on the unusual bottle (fig. 10), with its sophisticated shading to depict volume and depth – aspects not relevant in traditional Chinese painting – required an immense colour range. *Falangcai* vessels were individually painted in very small numbers and tend to be unique or to come in pairs. Sir Percival's group is the most important after that in the National Palace Museum, Taipei.

Meanwhile, the Jingdezhen imperial kilns, supervised by a sequence of able officials, revived ancient models and techniques to create contemporary styles. Under the Yongzheng emperor, Tang Ying (AD 1682–1756) also developed painting on a porcelain 'canvas'. Nature scenes were 'wrapped' all around a vessel or extended from the outside to the inside to prompt the viewer to handle the object, as if unrolling a scroll painting. From the kilns' vast output Sir Percival made only a small selection, yet these are some of the most beautiful examples painted in the *doucai* (no. 43) and *fencai* (粉彩, 'powder colours', known in the West as *famille rose*) palettes (no. 44 and fig. 9 right). In the Qianlong reign, Jingdezhen's potters exploited every technique and colour ever invented, which left little for their successors to explore.

This brief overview can in no way do full justice to a collection as magnificent as Sir Percival's. Many fascinating

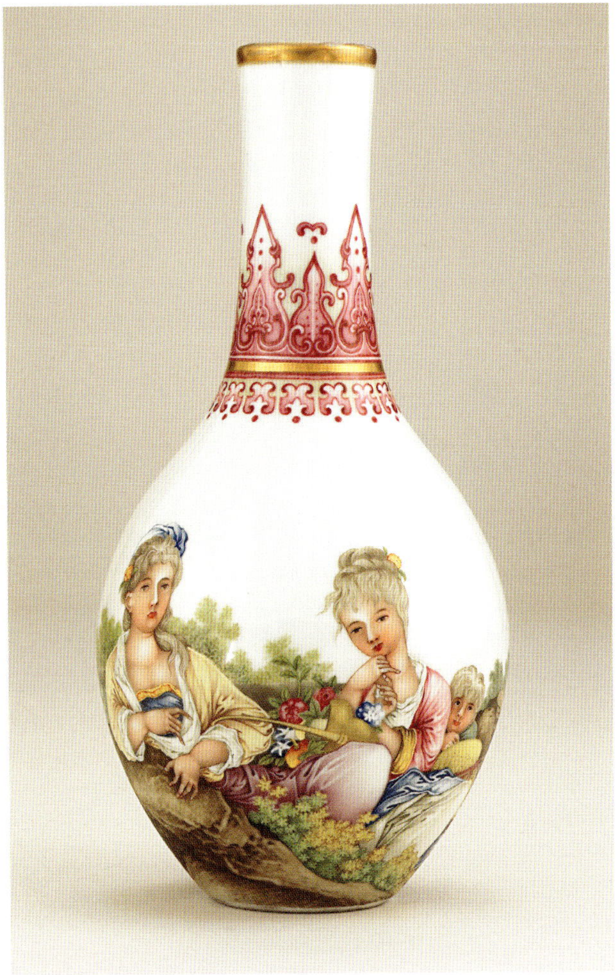

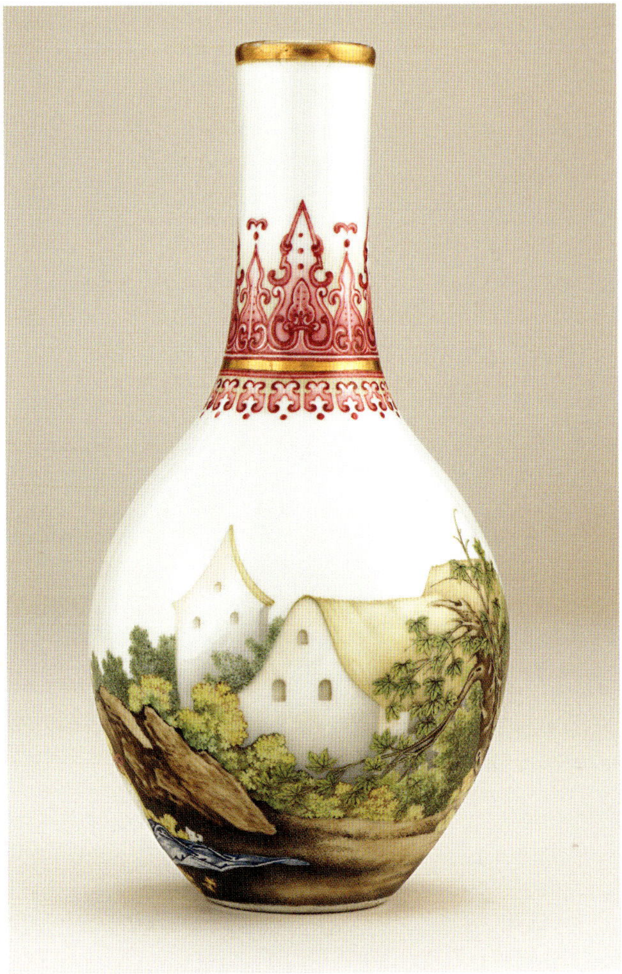

aspects have had to be ignored here and readers familiar with all its highlights will undoubtedly miss 'old friends' in the following selection. The choice has been difficult, but the authors hope it conveys an idea of the marvels and pleasures the Sir Percival David collection holds in store and will thus inspire frequent visits to the Sir Joseph Hotung Centre for Ceramic Studies.

Fig. 10 (PDF A818)
Porcelain bottle painted with ladies in French rococo style
Jingdezhen kilns, Jiangxi province, and Beijing Palace Workshops
Qing dynasty, red enamel Qianlong mark and period, AD 1736–95
Height 20.5 cm

1. Several Westerners were actively collecting fine Chinese porcelains in China in the nineteenth century, well before the demise of the Qing dynasty. C. Oswald Liddell had acquired pieces directly from the imperial family already prior to 1900 (see Stacey Pierson, *Collectors, Collections and Museums: The field of Chinese ceramics in Britain, 1560–1960*, Bern, Peter Lang, 2007, p. 99); and a public sale of over three hundred lots of 'Furniture and Embellishments from the Imperial Palace, Peking', some of them 'disposed of by the imperial family last spring', was conducted in 1917 by the American Art Association in New York.
2. According to Lady David, Sir Percival bought one such collateral deposit of some fifty pieces in the late 1920s from the 'Yuin Yeh Bank', presumably the Yien Yieh Commercial Bank, or Yanye Yinhang ['Salt Industry Bank'] (see Lady David, 'Introduction' in Rosemary E. Scott, *Percival David Foundation of Chinese Art*, London, University of London, 1989, p. 10, and Jeannette Shambaugh Elliot with David Shambaugh, *The Odyssey of China's Imperial Art Treasures*, Seattle, University of Washington Press, 2005, p. 154, note 15). Items reputedly from imperial holdings came also indirectly via other collectors such as Liddell, De Forest and LeBlond.
3. Sotheby's London, 6 June 1935, lot 89.
4. R.L. Hobson, *A Catalogue of Chinese Pottery and Porcelain in the Collection of Sir Percival David Bt FSA*, London, 1934.
5. The terms 縹 [*piao*], denoting the clear bluish-green colour of nature, and 瓷 [*ci*], denoting high-fired stoneware or porcelain, are used to describe a wine vessel in a poem by Pan Yue (AD 247–300); see Rose Kerr and Nigel Wood, *Science and Civilisation in China*, vol. 5: *Chemistry and chemical technology*, part XII: *Ceramic technology*, Cambridge, Cambridge University Press, 2004, p. 11.
6. See Nigel Wood, 'Plate tectonics and Chinese ceramics: New insights into the origins of China's raw materials', *Taoci* no. 1, October 2000, pp. 15–24, and Kerr and Wood, *op. cit.*, pp. 49–55.
7. Korean potters made white porcelains from the fifteenth century onwards, but in very small quantities; Japanese porcelain became available in the seventeenth century, but only in the eighteenth century, when Böttger in Germany developed the first Western porcelains, did its manufacture spread worldwide.
8. Donations to the Buddha bone relic in the Famen Temple near Xi'an up until the year AD 874 included some green-glazed Yue wares among a profusion of gold and silverware.
9. The cargo of the Belitung wreck that sank in the early ninth century off Indonesia, probably on its way to Iran, comprised over 60,000 pieces of Chinese stoneware; the first Mesopotamian copies of Tang white wares also date from about this period.
10. For the geographic identification see Rosemary Scott quoting Li Huibing in *Imperial Taste: Chinese ceramics from the Percival David Foundation*, catalogue of an exhibition organized by the Los Angeles County Museum of Art, San Francisco, 1989, p. 24; 會稽 [*kuaiji*] is, however, an alternative form of 會計[*kuaiji*], a term used for the Palace Accounts Office; see *Zhongwen da cidian [The Encyclopedic Dictionary of the Chinese Language]*, ed. Chang Chi-yun, Taipei, Zhonghua Xueshuyuan Yinhang, 1973–5, vol. 4, p. 6700, and Charles O. Hucker, *A Dictionary of Official Titles in Imperial China*, Stanford University Press, 1985, p. 283.
11. Evelyn S. Rawski and Jessica Rawson, *China: The Three Emperors 1662–1795*, catalogue of an exhibition organized by the Royal Academy of Arts, London, 2005–6, cat. no. 173, penultimate image.
12. The dating controversy is discussed in Li Baoping, 'Numbered Jun Wares: Controversies and new kiln site discoveries', *Transactions of the Oriental Ceramic Society*, vol. 71, London, 2008, pp. 65–77. At court, Jun ware flower vessels may still have been in use in the early eighteenth century, as suggested by a court painting of a palace interior commissioned by the future Yongzheng emperor; see Rawski and Rawson, *op. cit.*, cat. no. 173, last image.

Chronology

Neolithic period	*c.* 7th–early 1st millennium BC
Shang dynasty	16th century–*c.* 1050 BC
Zhou dynasty	*c.* 1050–221 BC
Qin dynasty	221–206 BC
Han dynasty	206 BC–AD 220
Three Kingdoms	AD 220–265
Jin dynasty	AD 265–420
Southern and Northern Dynasties	AD 420–589
Sui dynasty	AD 581–618
Tang dynasty	AD 618–907
Liao dynasty	AD 907–1125
Five Dynasties	AD 907–960
Song dynasty	AD 960–1279
Northern Song	AD 960–1127
Southern Song	AD 1127–1279
Jin dynasty	AD 1115–1234
Yuan dynasty	AD 1279–1368

Ming dynasty	AD 1368–1644
Hongwu	AD 1368–1398
Yongle	AD 1403–1424
Xuande	AD 1426–1435
Zhengtong	AD 1436–1449
Jingtai	AD 1450–1456
Tianshun	AD 1457–1464
Chenghua	AD 1465–1487
Hongzhi	AD 1488–1505
Zhengde	AD 1506–1521
Jiajing	AD 1522–1566
Longqing	AD 1567–1572
Wanli	AD 1573–1620
Tianqi	AD 1621–1627
Chongzhen	AD 1628–1644
Qing dynasty	AD 1644–1911
Shunzhi	AD 1644–1661
Kangxi	AD 1662–1722
Yongzheng	AD 1723–1735
Qianlong	AD 1736–1795
Jiaqing	AD 1796–1820
Daoguang	AD 1821–1850
Xianfeng	AD 1851–1861
Tongzhi	AD 1862–1874
Guangxu	AD 1875–1908
Xuantong	AD 1909–1911

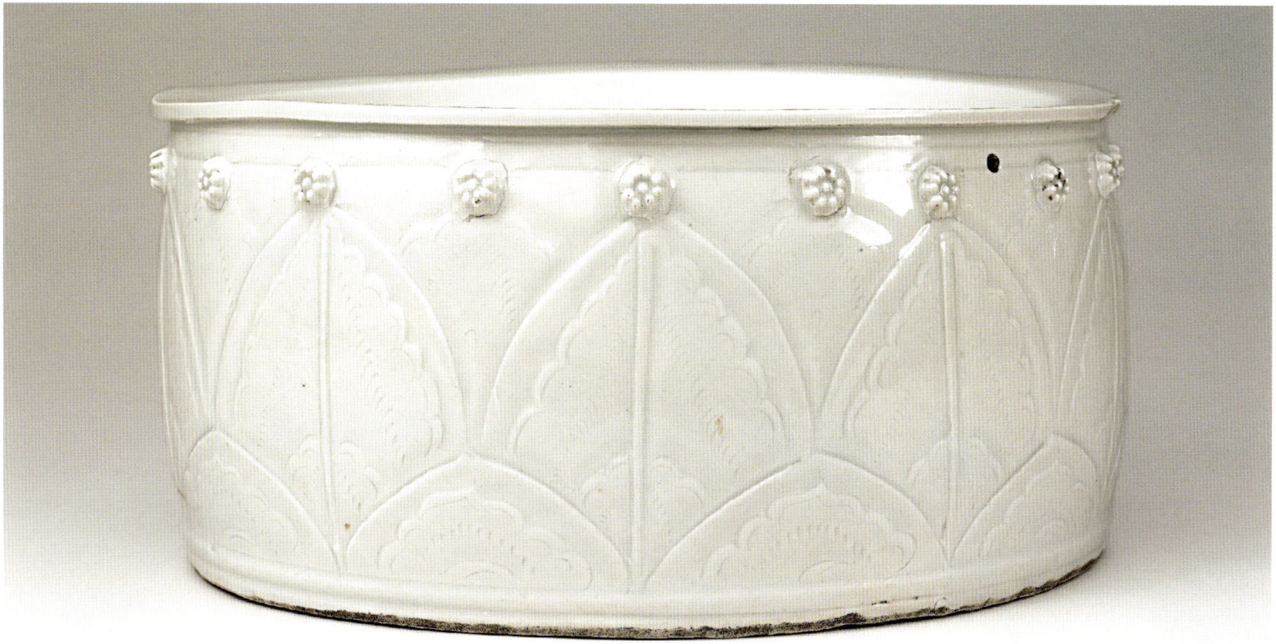

1 Drum-shaped bowl
Xing ware 邢窯
Neiqiu or Lincheng county, Hebei province
河北省，内丘縣 或者 臨城縣
Tang dynasty, about AD 800–907
Height 12.3 cm; diameter 26.5 cm
PDF 182

Buddhism, which originated in India, flourished in China during the fourth and fifth centuries AD, and its spread generated a new philosophy and a need for new paraphernalia for its rituals and ceremonies. This equipment often had shapes of Indian origin or, as in this case, was decorated with motifs originating in India.

Overlapping lotus petals, a common Buddhist motif, are carved around the sides of the bowl. Its drum-like shape may allude to the use of drums to call temple worshippers. A series of bosses around the rim suggest studs used for fastening the skin on an actual drum. Buddhist devotees may have used this vessel, which has a shallow bowl inside, as an alms bowl or for setting pure water on an altar. Chinese writers praised Xing white wares in historical texts, style treatises and poetry. The scholar Lu Yu (陸羽, AD 733–804) likened Xing wares to silver or snow in the first monograph on tea, 茶經 [*Chajing*, 'The Tea Classic'] written about AD 760–80. Xing ware can be hard to distinguish from Ding ware but generally it shows a colder bluer tone through its transparent glaze.

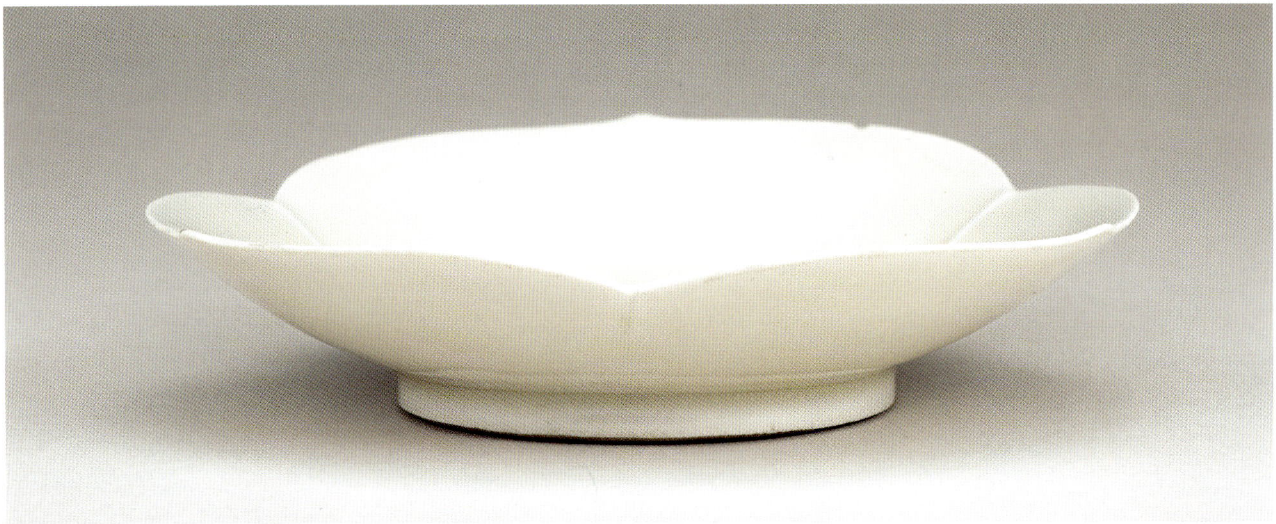

2 Trilobate dish with ivory glaze
Xing or Ding ware 邢窯或者定窯
Neiqiu/Lincheng or Quyang county, Hebei province
河北省，内丘縣 或者 臨城縣 或者 曲陽縣
Five Dynasties to early Northern Song dynasty, about AD 907–1000
Height 2.9 cm; diameter 13.4 cm
PDF 173

Craftsmen worked off-white local clay on a wheel and shaved the body down to create a fine dish with a rim in three brace bracket lobes. Contemporary Northern Song (AD 960–1127) silver- and lacquerware makers also used this flower-like form. Potters first added three radiating slip lines, then covered the dish with transparent glaze and fired it in the kiln protected within a rough clay container called a saggar, lined with sand, which is why traces of grit can be found stuck to its foot ring. Ding wares seldom bear inscriptions except for some high-quality vessels marked 官 [*guan*, 'official'] or 新官 [*xinguan*, 'new official']. Although the present dish is of this official quality, its base is instead incised 會稽 [*kuaiji*]. R.L. Hobson (1872–1941), former Keeper of the British Museum's Asian collections, first published this dish in 1934 and translated the inscription as *Kuiji* (an ancient southern Chinese place name that equates to Shaoxing in modern Zhejiang province). However, a new interpretation of these characters is proposed by Regina Krahl. 稽 [*ji*, 'to examine into'] was then an alternate character for 計 [*ji*, 'to calculate']. 會 may be read *hui* or *kui* but is also read *kuai*. 會計 [*Kuaiji*] is an abbreviation for 會計司 [*Kuaiji si*, 'Palace Accounts Office']. This makes more sense as an official ware made for the Palace Accounts Office. The characters were incised before firing, which precludes the possibility of it being a later inscription.

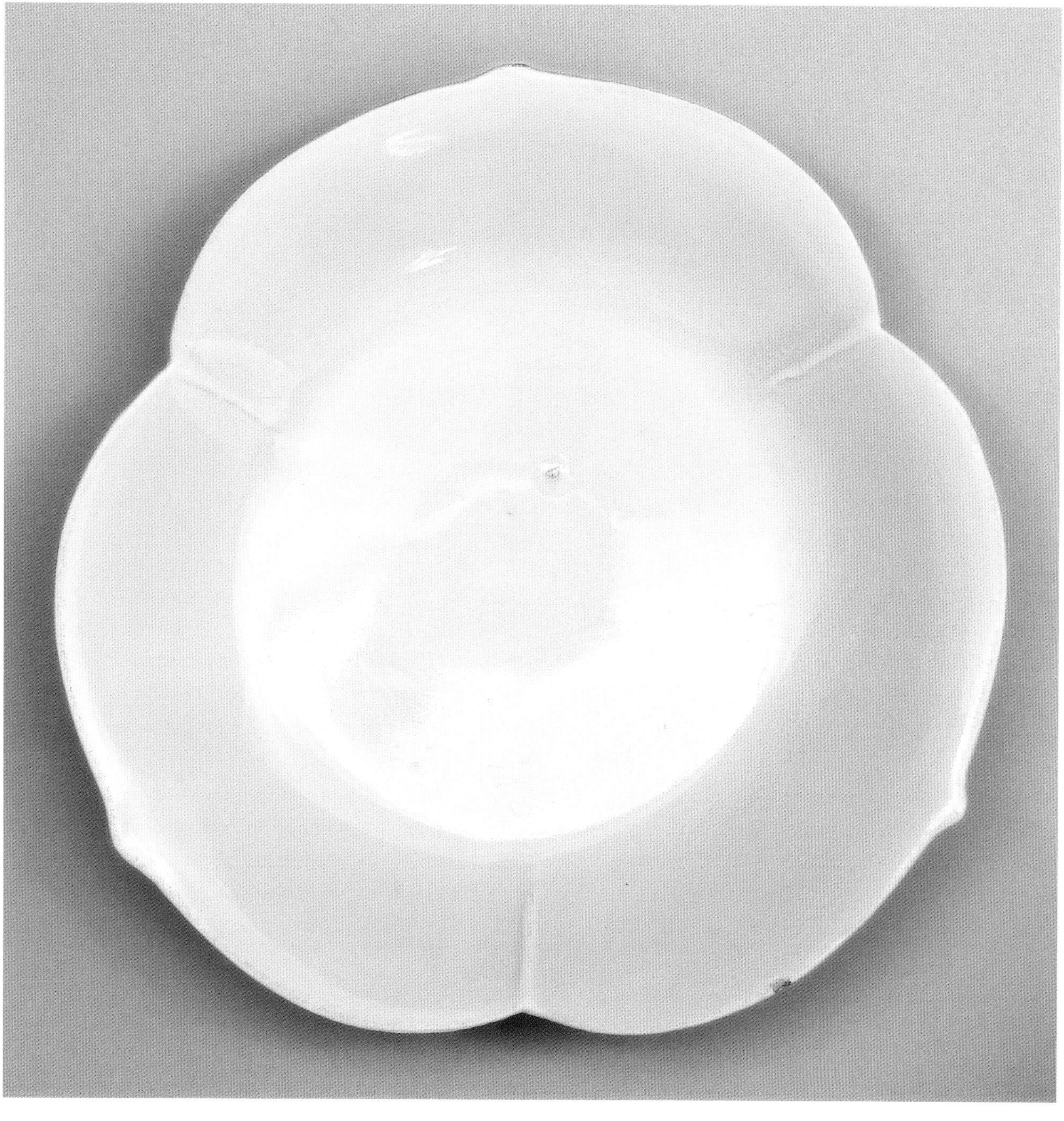

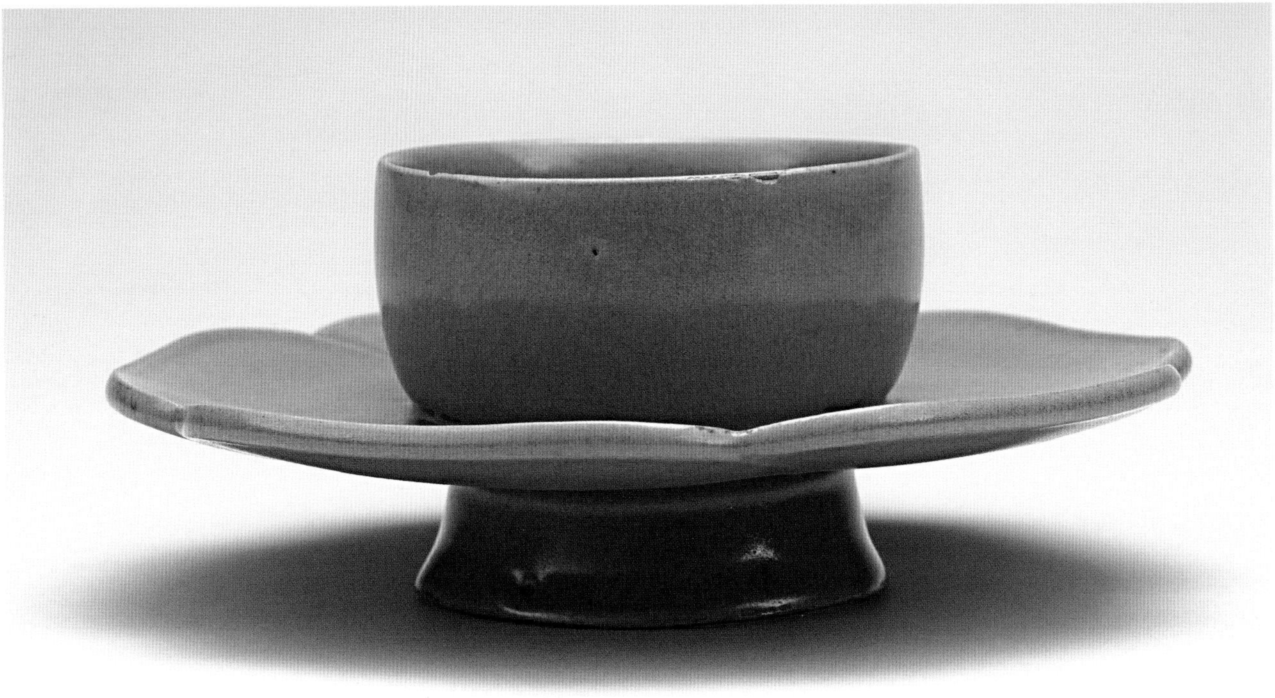

3 Flower-shaped bowl stand
Ru ware 汝窯
Qingliangsi, Baofeng county, Henan province 河南省, 寶豐縣, 清涼寺
Northern Song dynasty, about AD 1086–1125
Height 6.5 cm; diameter 17 cm
PDF 81

This stand is shaped like a small bowl, with a wide, five-petal flange and a high, flared foot. It was fired on its foot on a support with five prongs that have left five oval spur marks. Contemporary Song lacquer-, gold- and silver-workers made similar bowl stands. The design is inspired by a mallow flower with five petals. Here the idea of overlapping petals is suggested by using raised slip lines to outline the edges of each petal beneath the crackled celadon glaze. A similar bowl stand has been excavated at the Qingliangsi site in Baofeng county, Henan, where the present piece was probably made. Members of the Northern Song imperial court used such stands to support bowls of various materials for drinking tea. Korean potters supplying the Goryeo court with high-quality ceramics in the twelfth century made close copies of such Ru wares. Korean celadons and Chinese Ru wares have chemically similar glazes, suggesting an early international exchange of technology.

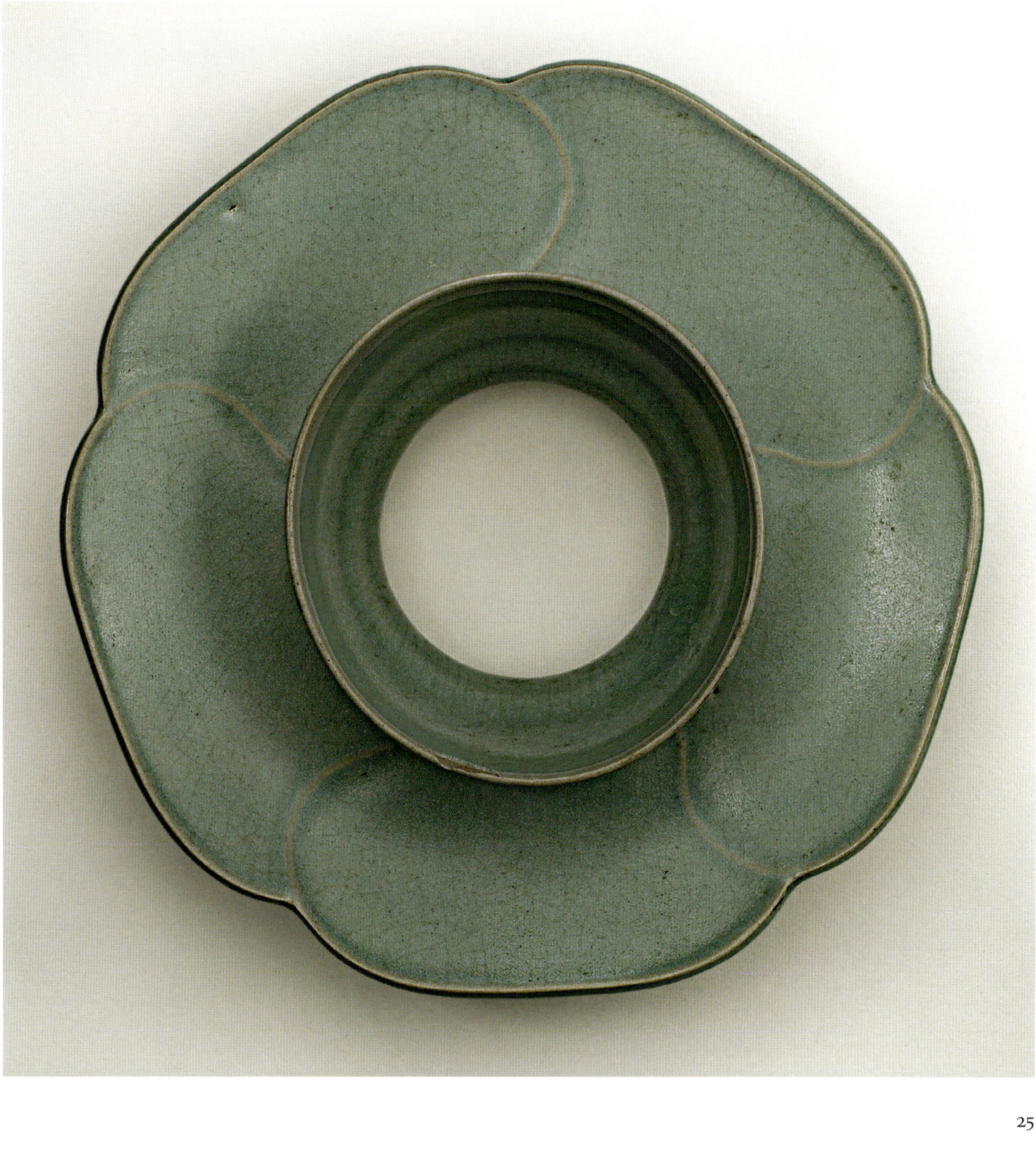

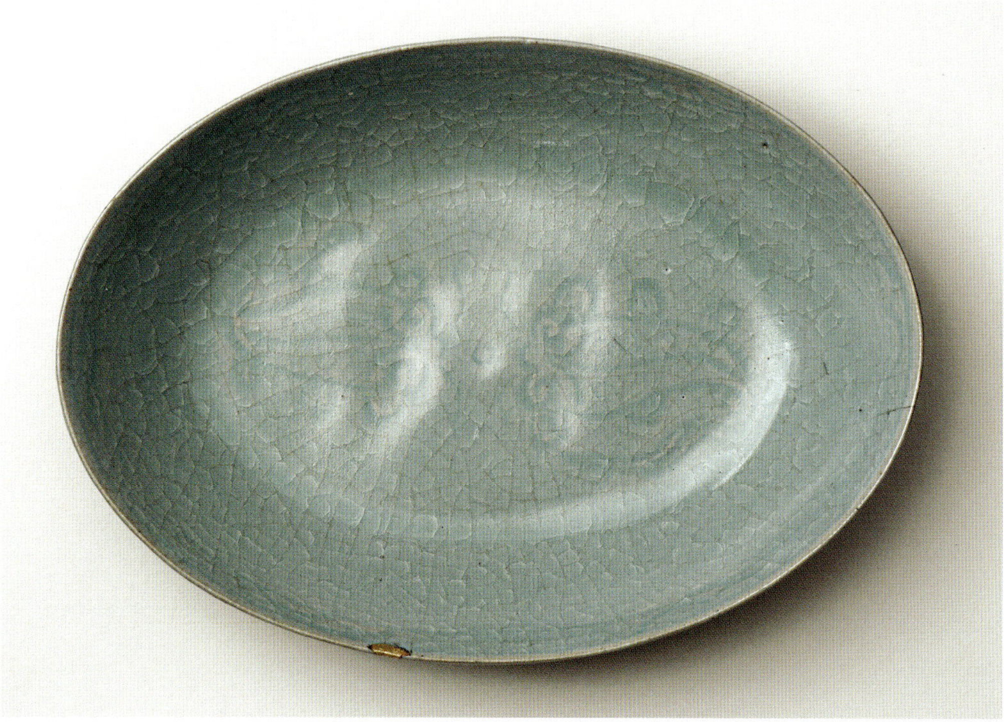

4 Oval brush-washer with two incised fish
Ru ware 汝窯
Qingliangsi, Baofeng county, Henan province 河南省,
寶豐縣, 清涼寺
Northern Song dynasty, about AD 1086–1125
Height 2.9 cm; diameter 14.5 cm
PDF 76

Craftsmen in Henan achieved a technical triumph in making this thinly potted brush-washer. They fully glazed the brush-washer before firing it on a support with three prongs that have left just three tiny unglazed 'sesame seed' marks within a depressed circular area on the base. Inside, two fish, a rebus for abundance, are incised in the clay beneath the glaze. Many connoisseurs regard Ru wares as the finest of all Chinese ceramics. Ru ware, characterized by its fine blue-grey-green, lightly crackled glaze, was made for only a short period for the Northern Song court from AD 1086 to 1106 or to 1125, and very few examples survive today outside the kiln sites. Both the oval form of this brush-washer and its incised decoration make it incredibly rare even within this exceptional group. Sherds of related wares have been excavated at Qingliangsi, a Ru ware production site in Baofeng county, Henan.

5 Bottle with copper rim mount
Ru ware 汝窯
Qingliangsi, Baofeng county, Henan province 河南省，寶豐縣，清涼寺
Northern Song dynasty, about AD 1086–1125
Height 24.8 cm; diameter 15.6 cm
PDF 61

Ru wares have a slightly underfired (1200–1250°C), thin, pale-grey stoneware body, with a comparatively thick celadon glaze. Song dynasty authors describe this Ru glaze as containing powdered agate that was mined locally to the Qingliangsi kiln site. The fine bluish colour of this glaze is in fact caused by dissolved iron oxide together with very low levels of titanium dioxide. Titanium has a yellowing effect on glaze colour and usually encourages a green tone in most Chinese celadons. A yellow cast can also come from coal-firing but the Ru ware potters seem to have practised wood-firing, even though most north Chinese kilns at this time were fired with coal. Archaeologists discovered a related slim-necked vase with flared foot and mouth at the Qingliangsi kiln site. The present bottle's rim may have been repaired with copper to disguise a flaw or chip.

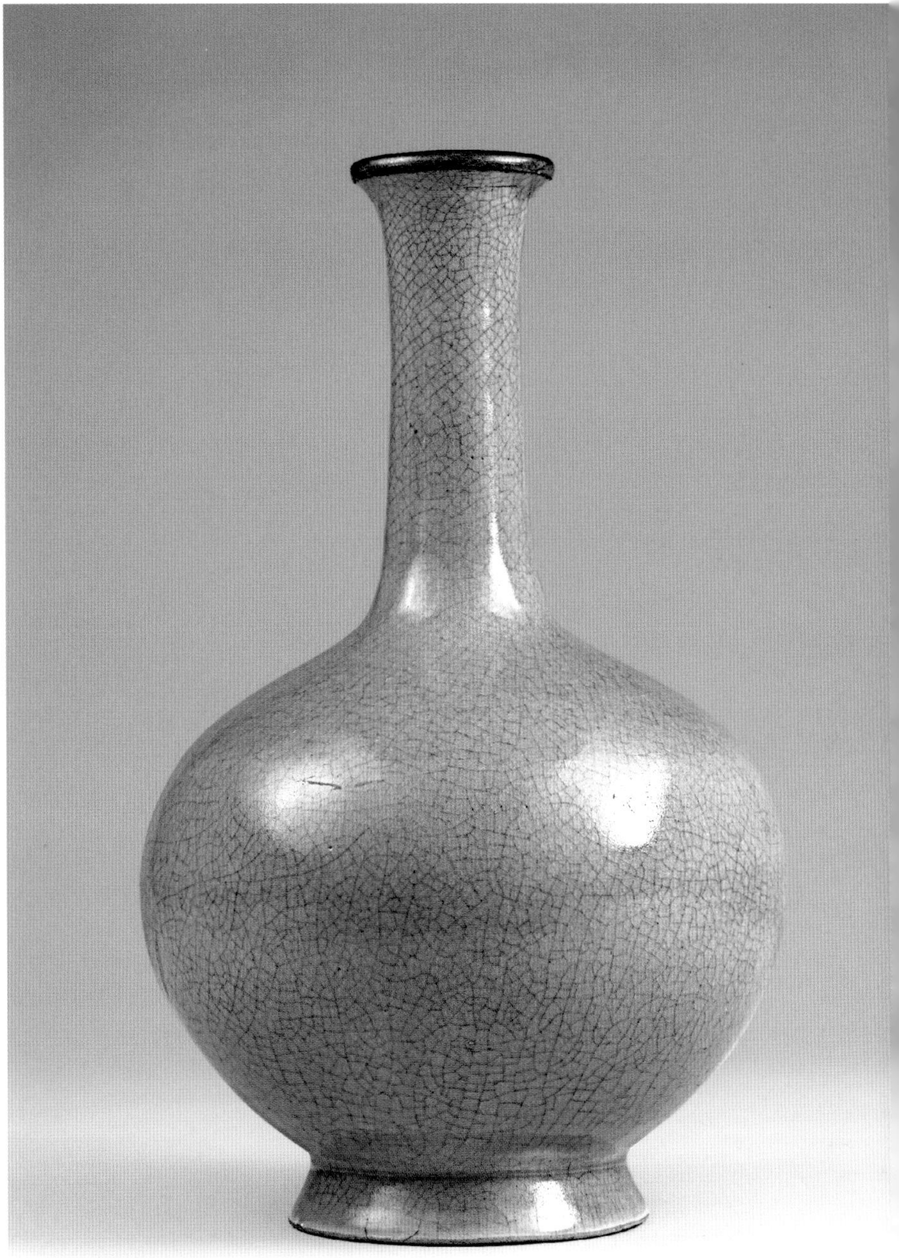

6 Incense burner with three cabriole legs
Ru ware 汝窯
Qingliangsi, Baofeng county, Henan province 河南省，寶豐縣，清涼寺
Northern Song dynasty, about AD 1086–1125
Height 15.3 cm; diameter 24.8 cm
PDF A44

This unusually large incense burner evokes antiquity through both its shape and its glaze. Potters modelled the cylindrical body, cabriole legs and carved horizontal line decoration after an antique bronze or lacquer container called 奩 (*lian*) made in the Warring States or Han dynasty period (475 BC–AD 220). The colour of the incense burner's crackled grey-blue-green glaze is suggestive of the appearance of ancient jades. In AD 1151, General Zhang Jun, a favoured official of the Southern Song emperor Gaozong (ruled AD 1127–62), presented the emperor with sixteen Ru ware ceramics, including a large and a small censer. The gift may have included an incense burner like this one. Archaeologists have discovered that, after the Song court moved south from Kaifeng to Hangzhou, potters made versions of this type of censer at the *guan* ['official'] ware kilns at Laohudong, Hangzhou.

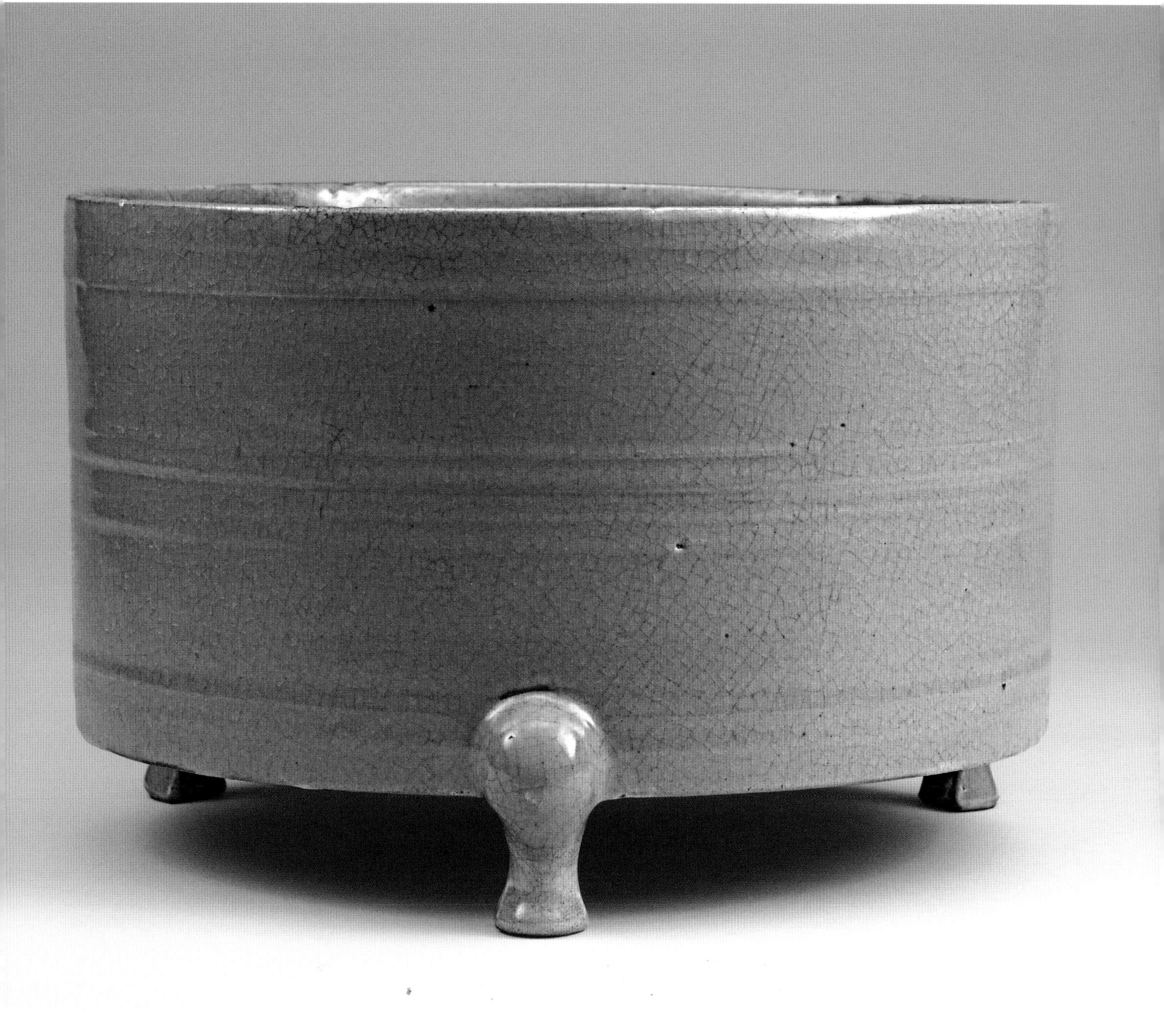

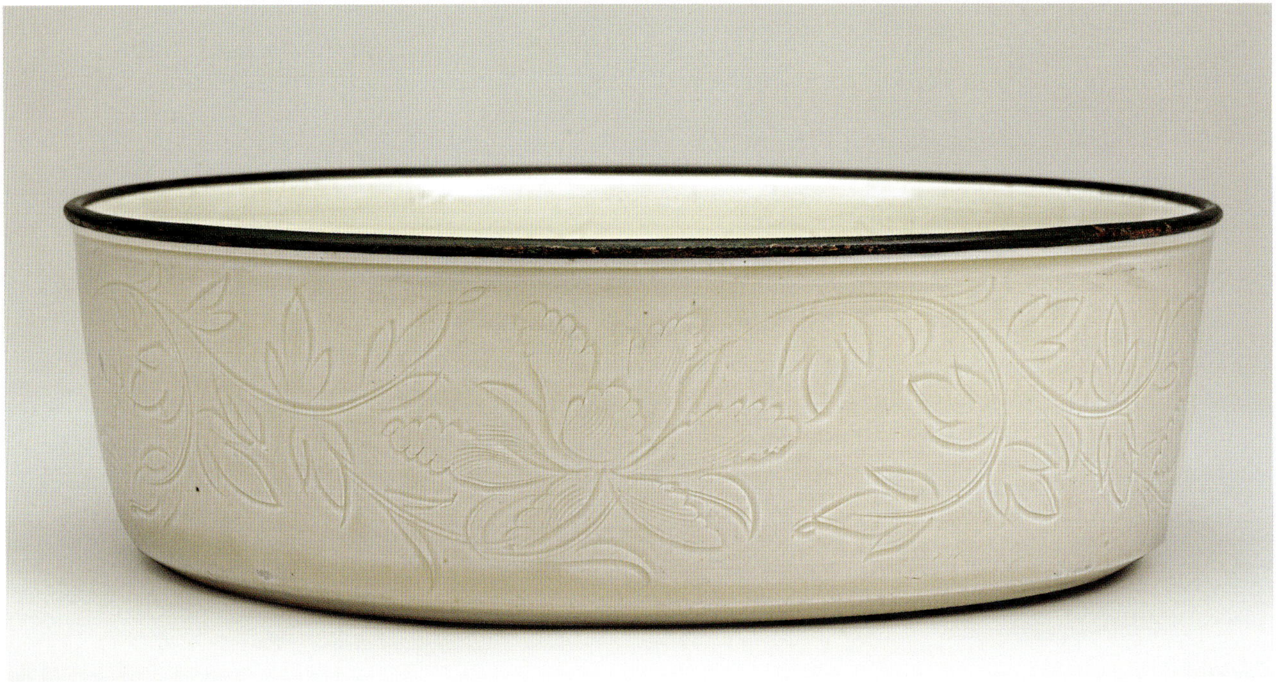

7 Basin with carved peonies and a copper rim
Ding ware 定窯
Quyang county, Hebei province 河北省，曲陽縣
Northern Song dynasty, about AD 1086–1127
Height 8.8 cm; diameter 27.7 cm
PDF 102

The shape of this basin is unusual for surviving Ding wares. It is incised with flowering peonies that have combed textured petals. The base of the basin is fully glazed. Between about AD 1086 and 1127 potters revolutionized firing methods at the Ding kilns and pioneered the technique of *fushao* (firing a vessel upside down on its rim instead of its base) in a stepped saggar. Kiln managers saved money on fuel by firing a greater number of pots at one time, stacking them in saggars. The main disadvantage was the coarse, unglazed mouth rim, which was cleaned free of glaze to avoid the vessel sticking to the saggar. Craftsmen used sheet copper, cut and heated to fit the rough rims, in order to hide this flaw. Historical accounts suggest that dressing the rim with metal actually enhanced the status of the clay vessel. Potters kept the Ding ware kilns in almost constant operation from the early eighth until the mid fourteenth century, benefiting from plentiful supplies of clay and coal and a river network to distribute the finished goods.

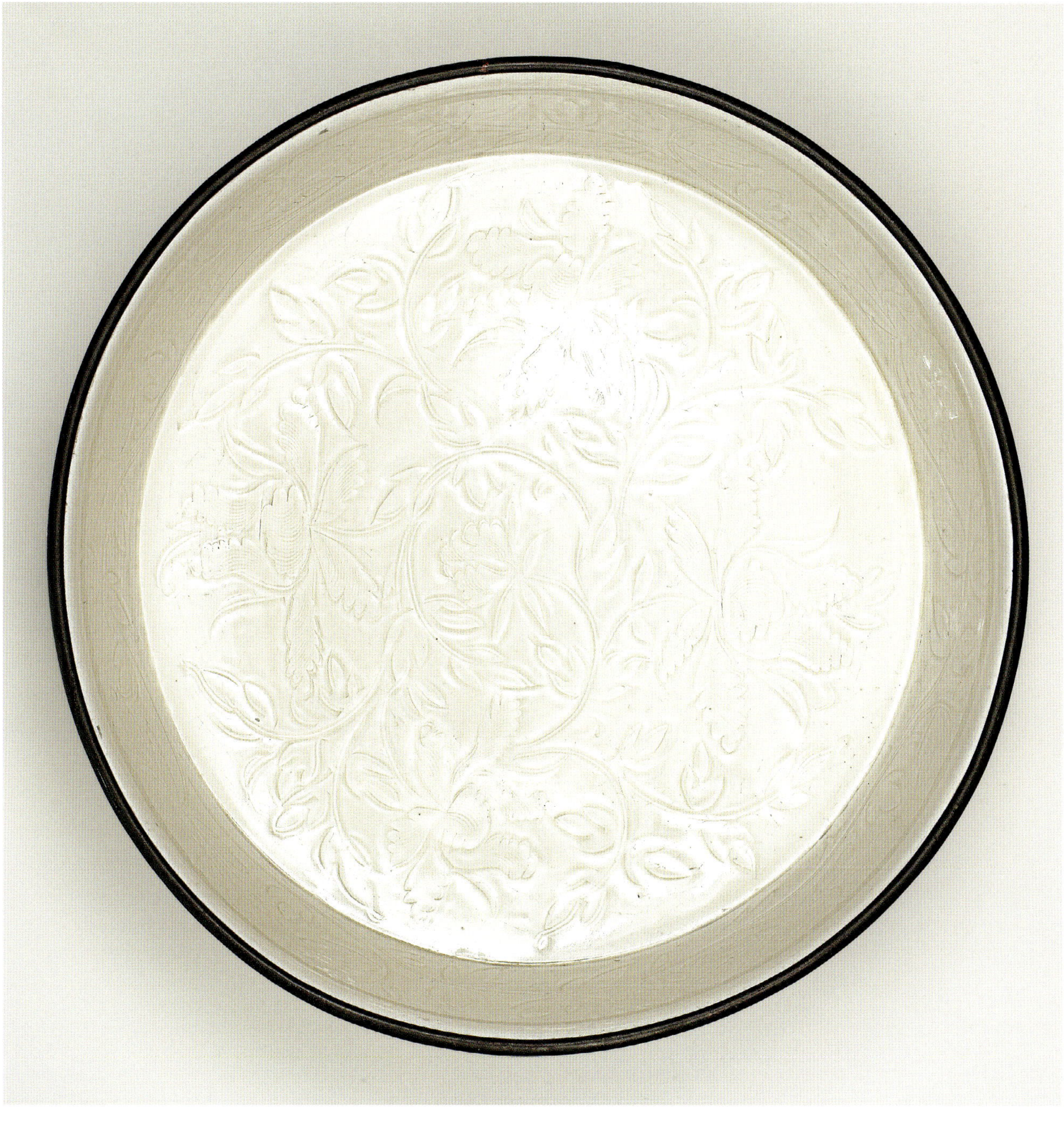

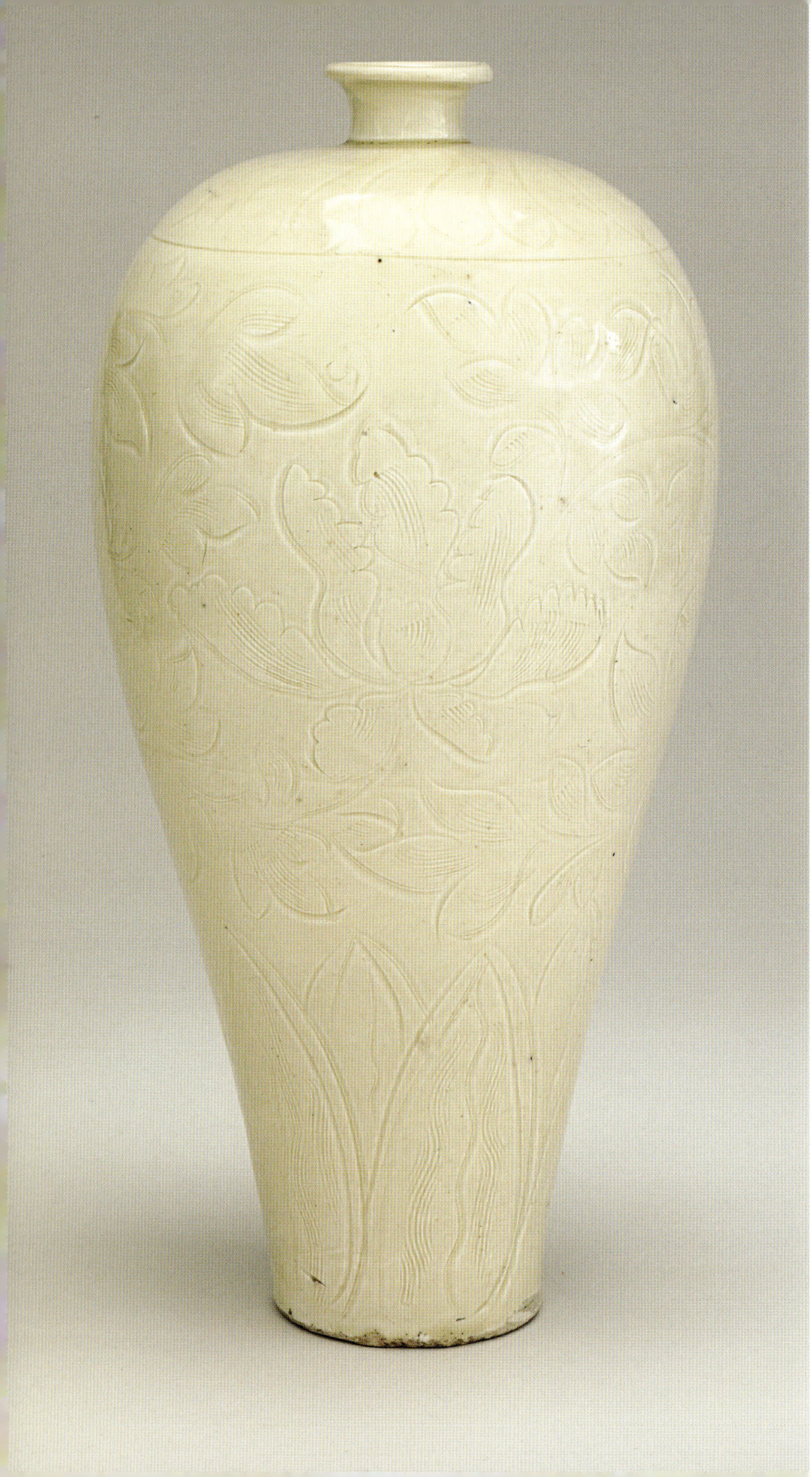

8 ***Meiping* vase with carved peonies**

Ding ware 定窯

Quyang county, Hebei province 河北省，曲陽縣

Northern Song dynasty, AD 960–1127

Height 36.5 cm

PDF 101

The form of this stoneware vase is extremely elegant. The runny ivory Ding glaze dribbles in streaks, like tears filling the combed and incised double outlines of the design. The *meiping* is decorated around the body with peony flowers, with overlapping lotus petals around the foot and with a reversed 'S' pattern around the shoulder. In the Northern Song potters fired Ding wares at high temperatures in the 1280–1320°C range in kilns shaped like giant *mantou* [steamed bread buns]. They used coal as fuel and the sulphur content of the coal, combined with the oxidizing atmosphere of the kiln, gave the ceramics an ivory tone. Local officials offered high-quality products such as this vase as tribute to the Northern Song court. The presence of Ding wares in monastery treasuries, palaces and noblemen's tombs testifies to their high status even when they were new. Officials from Dingzhou regulated Quyang county from the Tang dynasty (AD 618–906), which is why products of Quyang are known as Ding wares.

9 Box carved with peony flowers

Yaozhou ware 耀洲窯

Huangpuzhen, Tongchuan city, Shaanxi province 陝西省，銅川市，黃堡鎮

Northern Song dynasty, about AD 1000–1127

Height 9 cm; diameter 17.1 cm

PDF 244

This covered box has a light grey body of a fine compact texture and an even, olive-green coloured glaze. The makers deeply carved its decoration of four peony flowers, bordered by a band of leaf scroll, and petals around the flattened sides into the leather-hard clay. They added texture using a comb tool, and then dipped the box and cover into the liquid glaze that pooled in the grooves of the design, creating a contrasting dark and light floral pattern. Potters fired ceramics of this quality in saggars within a coal-fired kiln. Bureaucrats may have sent such items as tribute to the Northern Song court; merchants also traded Yaozhou wares widely. Archaeologists have unearthed examples of mostly poorer quality Yaozhou and related wares in many medieval sites in Asia, the Near East and East Africa. In the Song dynasty, the best kilns were located at Huangpu near modern Tongchuan city, which then was under the jurisdiction of Yaozhou county – hence their name.

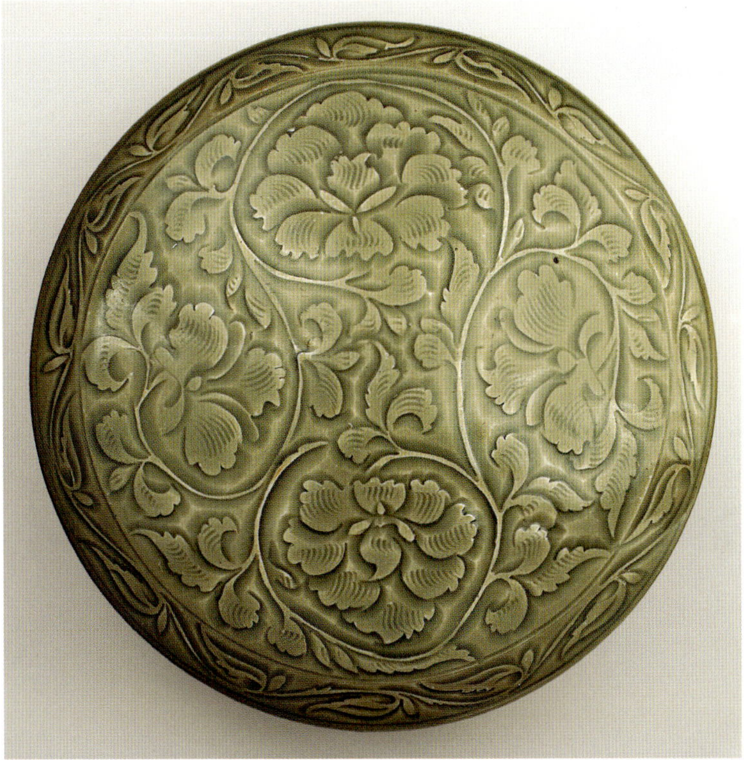

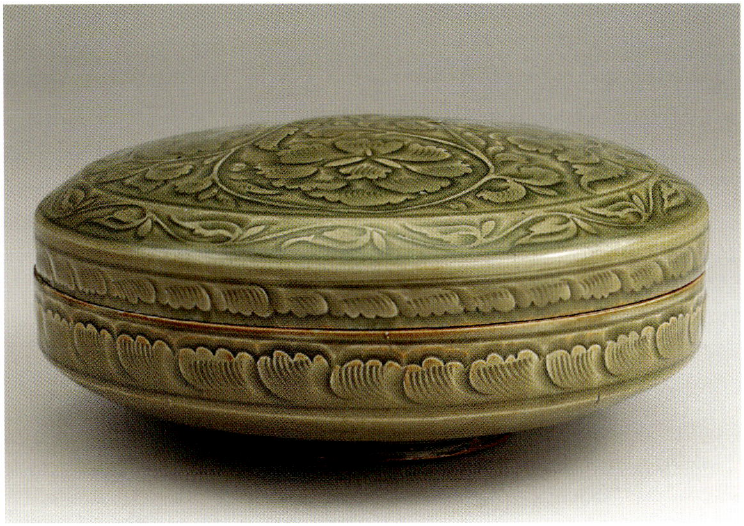

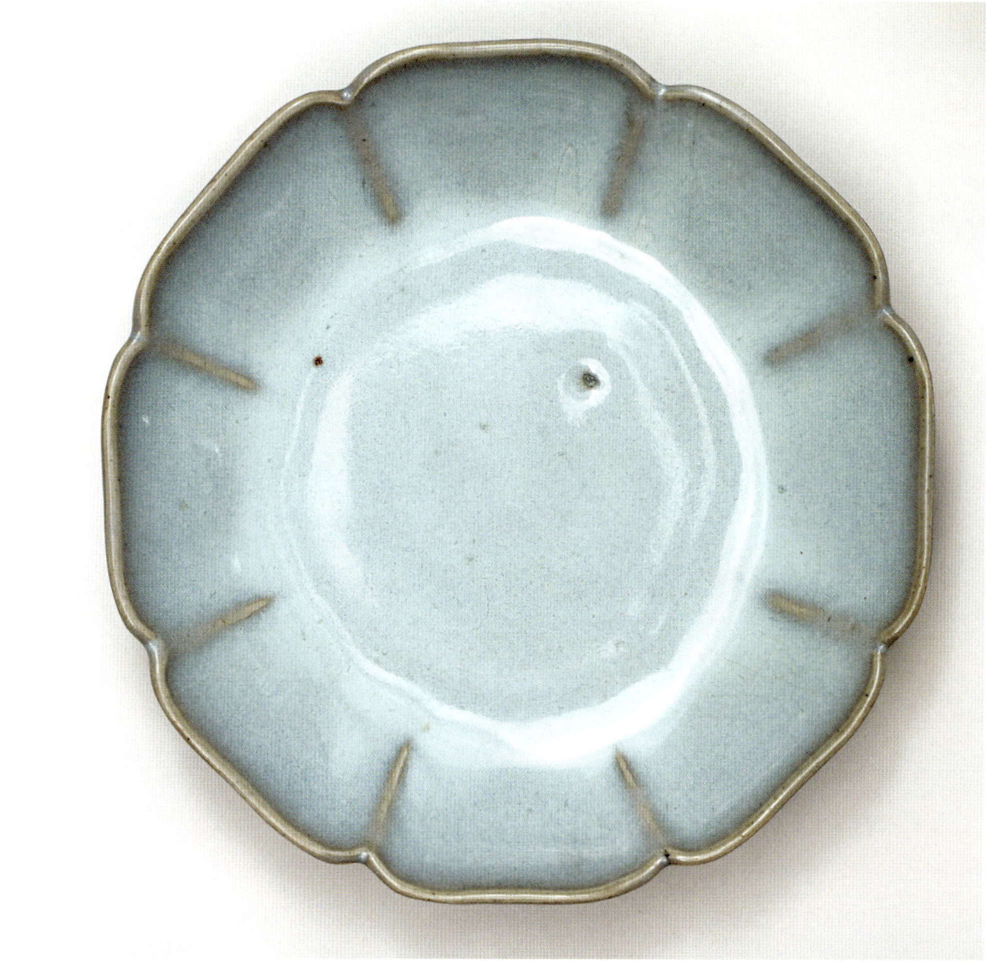

10 Eight-petal lobed dish
Jun ware 鈞窯
Yuxian, Henan province 河南省, 禹縣
Northern Song dynasty, about AD 1000–1127
Height 3.2 cm; diameter 13.4 cm
PDF A4

Jun wares of this fine quality and form are exceptionally rare. Potters threw the dish on a potter's wheel; then they created its distinct eight-petal flower shape using an indenting tool. Potters supported the dish on a three-pronged setter, and the base has three large, coarse spur marks showing where the setter was removed and where the glassy glaze has pooled. These spur marks are much larger and rougher than those left on imperial wares made at the northern Ru and southern *guan* kilns.

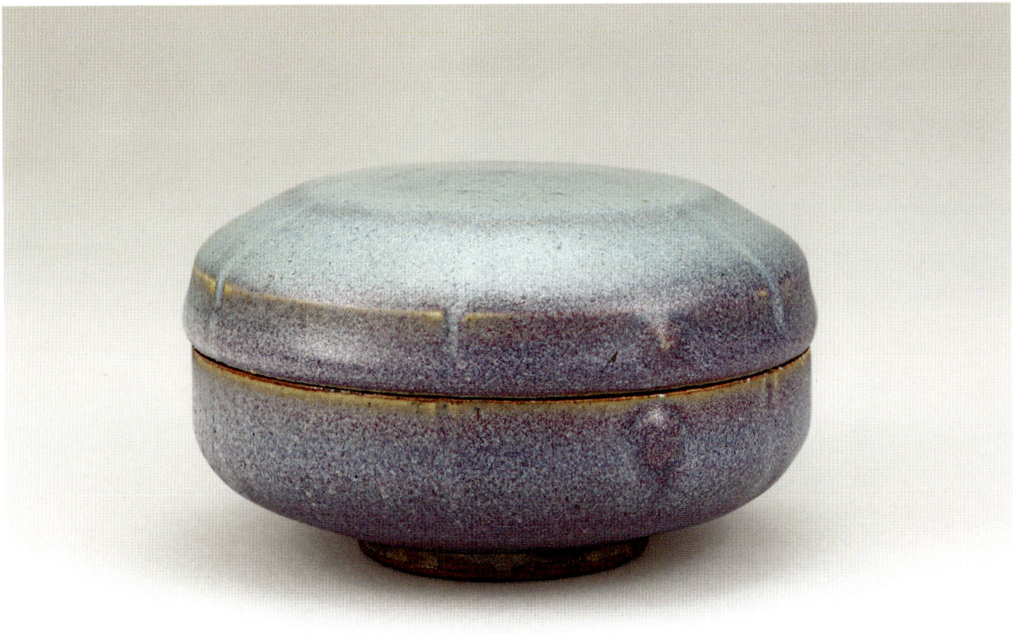

11 Box with faceted sides
Jun ware 鈞窯
Yuxian, Henan province 河南省，禹縣
Northern Song dynasty, about AD 1000–1127
Height 6.5 cm; diameter 11 cm
PDF 42

The form of this circular box with flat top and sides scored into six sections is also found in contemporary Northern Song silverware. It has small knobs of clay on the cover and tray beneath the glaze, which when lined up give the correct fit. The glaze on the tray and faceted sides of the cover are lavender while the cover's top and the inside of both halves of the box are sky blue. Where the glaze runs thin towards the edge of the lid, tray and foot, it becomes semi-transparent to olive green. Compared to contemporary Northern Song celadons such as Ru and Yaozhou wares, Jun wares have relatively coarse stoneware bodies. Jun wares are characterized by opalescent blue, purple or occasionally green glazes. Although some scholars believe a quantity of very fine Jun wares were sent as tribute to the Northern Song court, most of the output from the Jun kilns was made for non-imperial consumers and it was rarely exported. Small boxes such as this were probably used to store cosmetics, seal paste or incense. Jun wares were made in many kilns throughout Junzhou prefecture (modern Yuzhou or Yuxian) in Henan province.

12 Bottle with purple-splashed blue glaze
Jun ware 鈞窯
Yuxian, Henan province 河南省，禹縣
Northern Song dynasty, about AD 1000–1127
Height 29 cm
PDF 92

Northern Song dynasty potters were extremely skilled, as demonstrated by the technical difficulties of throwing horizontal clay sections on a wheel and luting these together to create this bottle's pear-shaped body and tall, slender neck that flares at the mouth. Potters decorated the dry, unfired glaze with copper-rich pigment to create a purple in-glaze splashed effect. Jun wares are not as well finished as Ru or *guan* wares. In this instance, craftsmen glazed the bottle's base inside the foot ring but only glazed inside the neck of the bottle, leaving the rest of the inside unglazed. Northern Song tomb murals show bottles of this shape being used to display a single flower stem but they may also have been used for decanting wine. Modern studio potters living almost a thousand years later, such as the British artist Bernard Leach (1887–1979), were inspired by the opalescent Jun stoneware glazes to create their own beautiful versions.

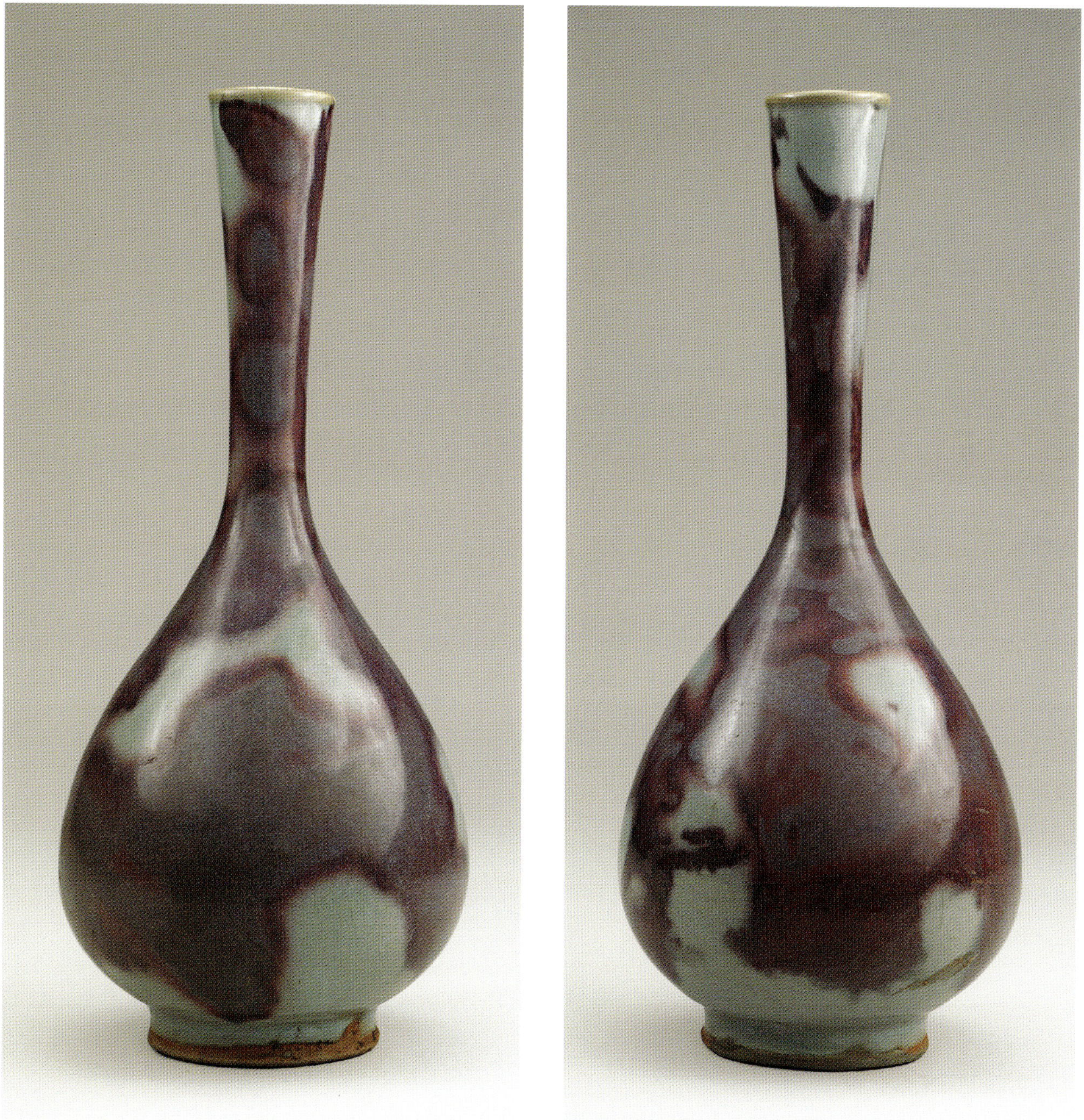

13 Eight-petal lobed dish

Guan ware 官窯

Hangzhou, Zhejiang province 浙江省，杭州市

Southern Song dynasty, AD 1127–1279

Height 3.9 cm; diameter 16.8 cm

PDF A46

In the twelfth century the Song imperial court lost control of northern China to the invading Jin army. In AD 1127 they fled from their capital in Bianjing (modern Kaifeng) and established a new centre of government south of the Yangzi River in Lin'an (modern Hangzhou). The Gaozong emperor (ruled AD 1127–62) established an official kiln there to recreate the northern Ru wares that the Song emperors admired so much. These *guan* [official] stonewares are characterized by a thin body made from dark clay and a beautiful thick, glassy, celadon glaze with tiny bubbles and a wide crackle that can appear reddish brown when the body shows through. Although superficially similar, the shape of this dish is much more refined than the Jun ware version (see no. 10). Each petal lobe is curved and indented to create a naturalistic mallow flower form. Similar dishes made of silver were recovered from the Southern Song dynasty hoard of gold- and silverwares at Pengzhou, Sichuan. The glazer has left his fingerprints in the glaze on the base, a tantalizing and rare trace of the craftsman's hand.

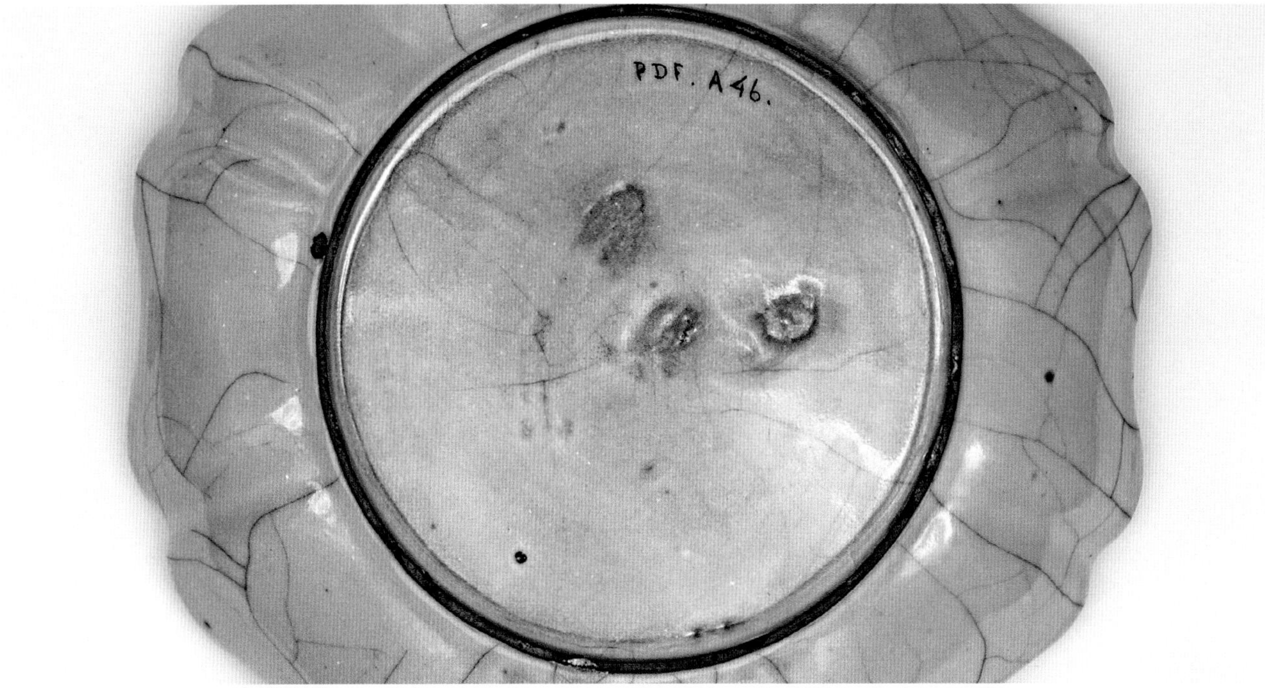

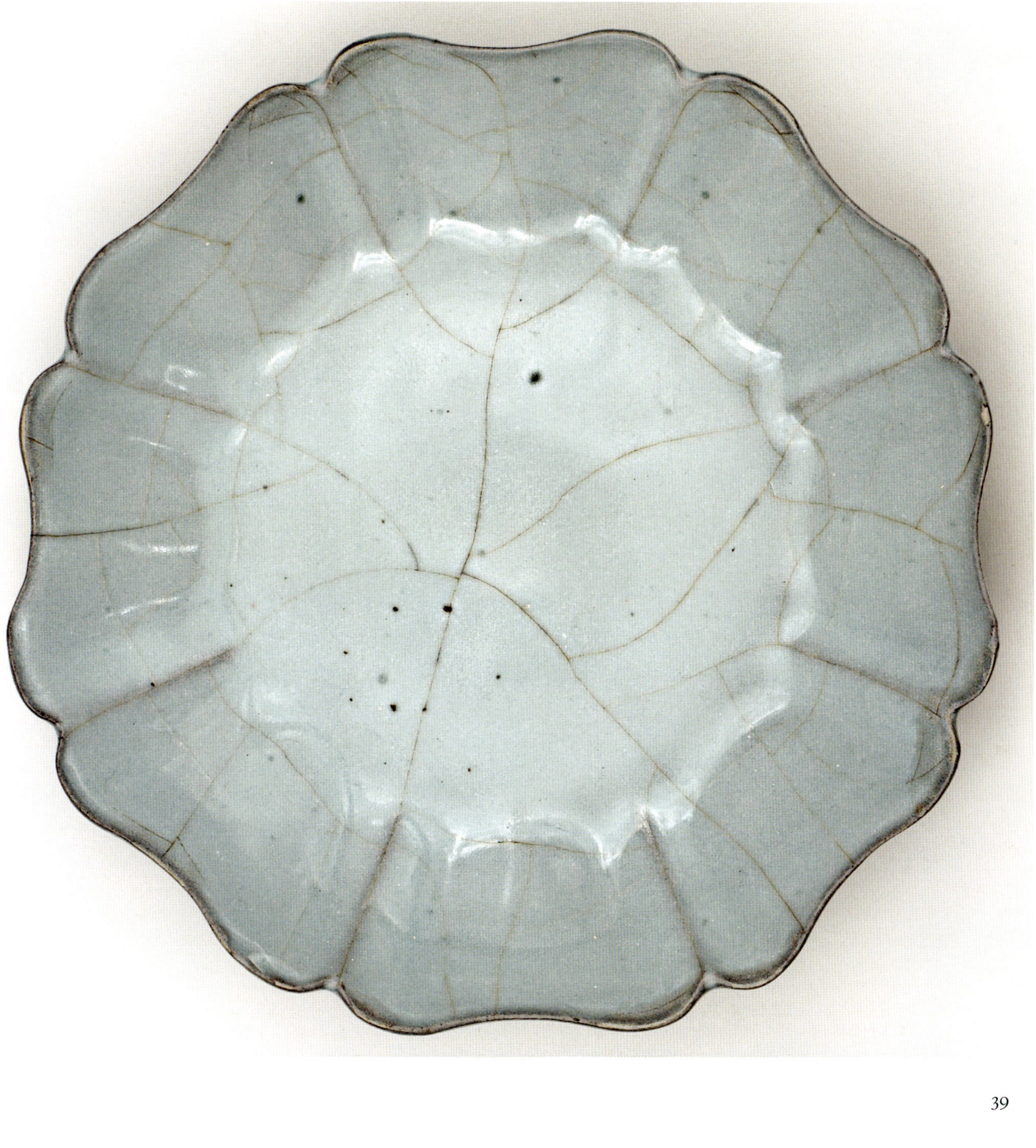

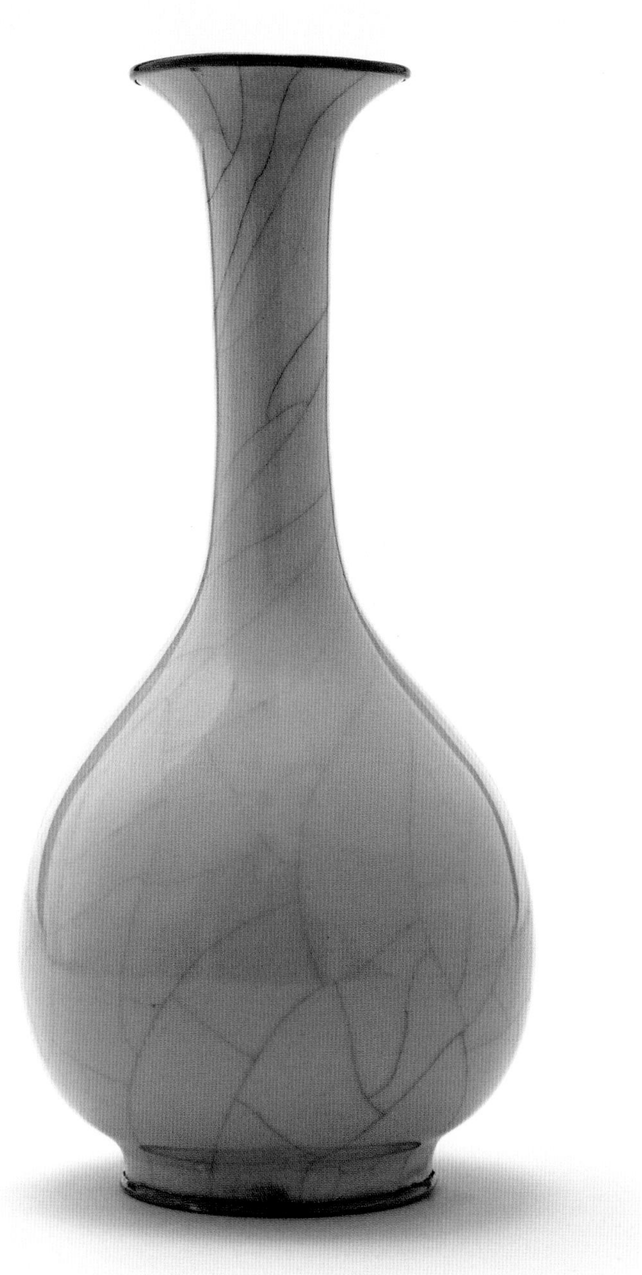

14 Bottle with copper-mounted rim and foot

Guan ware 官窯
Hangzhou, Zhejiang province 浙江省，杭州市
Southern Song dynasty, AD 1127–1279
Height 18 cm; diameter 8.5 cm
PDF 4

Potters made *guan* wares at the Laohudong [老虎洞] kiln site in Hangzhou. Scholars suggest this site may be the one described in historical texts as 修内司 [*xiuneisi*, 'Palace Maintenance Office'] or 内窯 [*neiyao*, 'Inner Kiln']. Most scholars believe the Laohudong kiln was set up before the Jiaotanxia [郊壇下] kiln. The emperor probably needed the new kiln to meet increasing demands for ceramic products for the Song court and, because there were physical restrictions on developing the Laohudong site, built the Jiaotanxia kiln. Craftsmen at both these production sites made ritual, table and ornamental wares for the imperial court. Archaeologists excavated sherds of copies of similar slender-necked bottles with pear-shaped bodies at the Jiaotanxia kiln site in the Fenghuang mountains [鳳凰山] near Hangzhou.

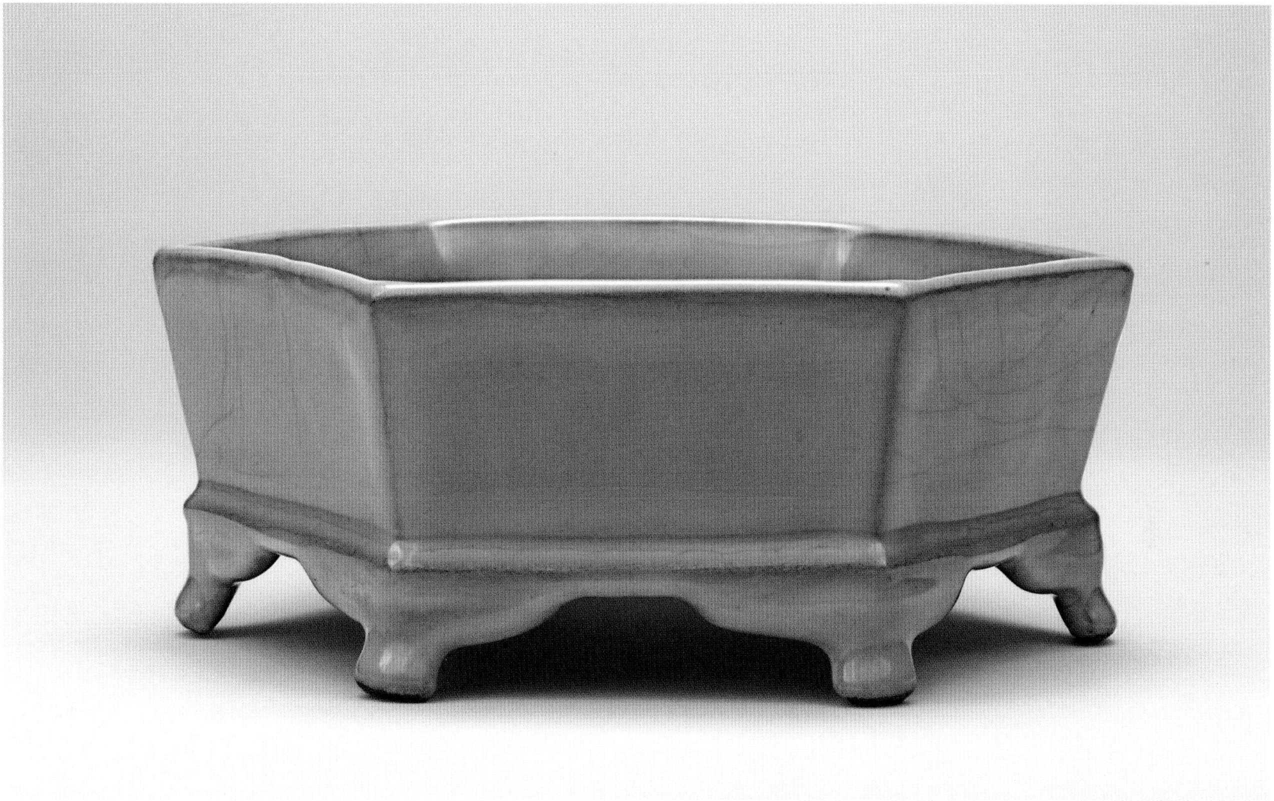

15 Hexagonal basin with six feet
Guan ware 官窯
Hangzhou, Zhejiang province 浙江省，杭州市
Southern Song dynasty, AD 1127–1279
Height 8.5 cm; diameter 21.5 cm
PDF 6

Writers described *guan* ware such as this basin as having 紫口鐵足 [*zikou tiezu*, 'purple mouth and iron foot'], referring to the dark purplish-grey body showing through the glaze where it has run thin at the rim and to the ferrous-brown colour of the unglazed feet. The shape of this deep hexagonal dish on six feet is extremely unusual in surviving Chinese ceramics of this period. Perhaps the Southern Song court commissioned it based on a metalwork vessel, for which straight edges and an angular profile would appear to be more natural than for a ceramic one. The use of the basin is unclear: possibly it was made for the emperor as a stand for a six-sided *guan* ware flowerpot with drilled drainage holes in the base and filled with soil to grow plants in. Alternatively it may have been used directly for growing bulbs.

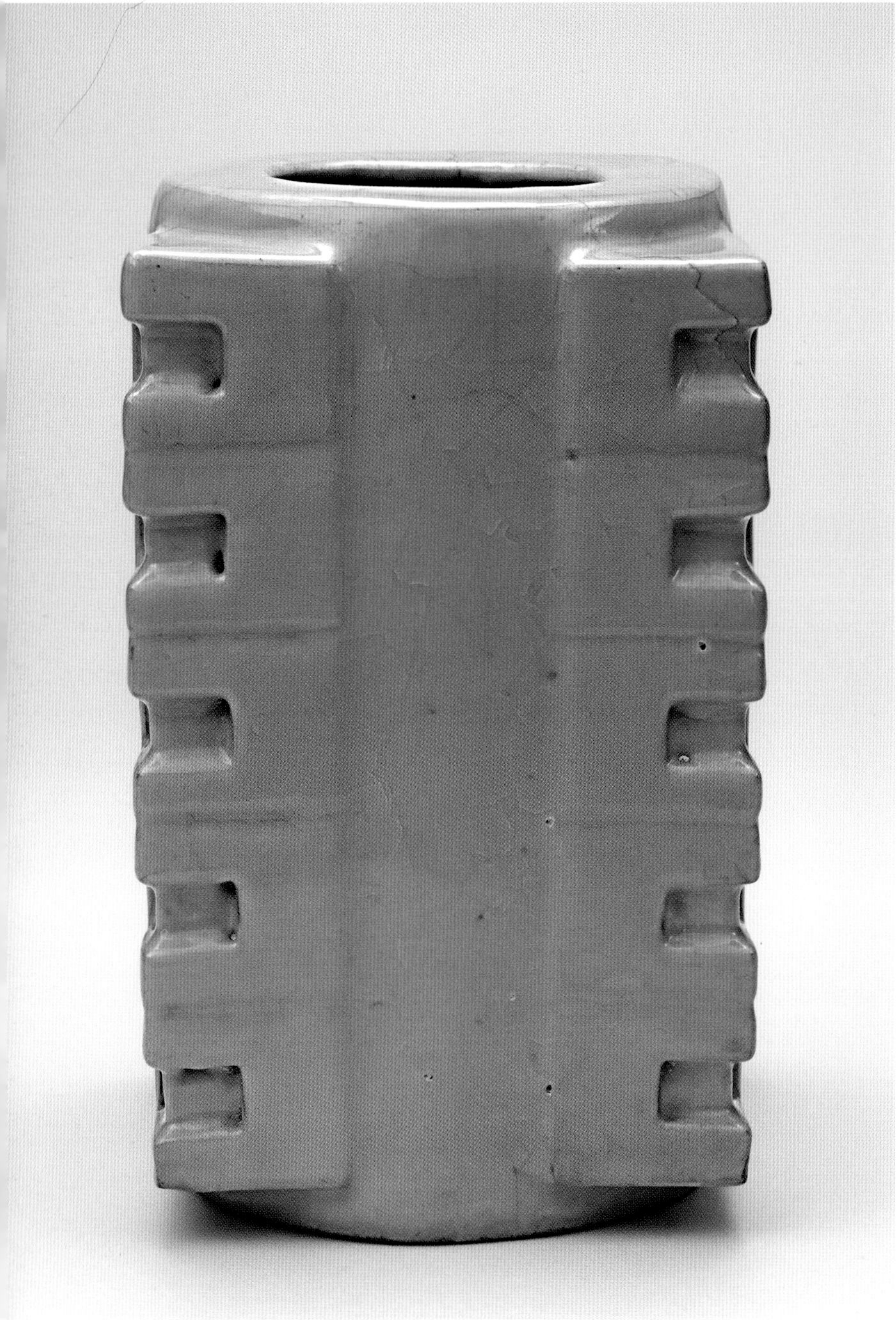

16 Vessel in the form of a *cong*
Guan ware 官窯
Hangzhou, Zhejiang province 浙江省，杭州市
Southern Song dynasty, AD 1127–1279
Height 22.6 cm; width 13.7 cm; depth 13.6 cm
PDF 99

In China's southeast, corresponding to modern Jiangsu and Zhejiang provinces, in the second and third millennia BC, jade carvers of the Liangzhu culture fashioned tubes of jade with square sides pierced by a circular opening called 琮 [*cong*]. Ancient people buried these with the corpse possibly as a sign of wealth and because they believed jade could protect the body. In the Song dynasty, educated men revived interest in antiques and excavated artefacts from the past. Scholars published manuals illustrating these historical jades and bronzes. Contemporary Song craftsmen reproduced their shapes in other materials, responding to commissions from wealthy clients, and the new users adapted the functions of the antique objects. Archaeologists have excavated archaistic *cong* made in a variety of materials in several Southern Song dynasty hoards including a bronze *cong* at the Pengzhou hoard and carved stone and celadon examples in the Jinyucun hoard of Suining city, both in Sichuan province.

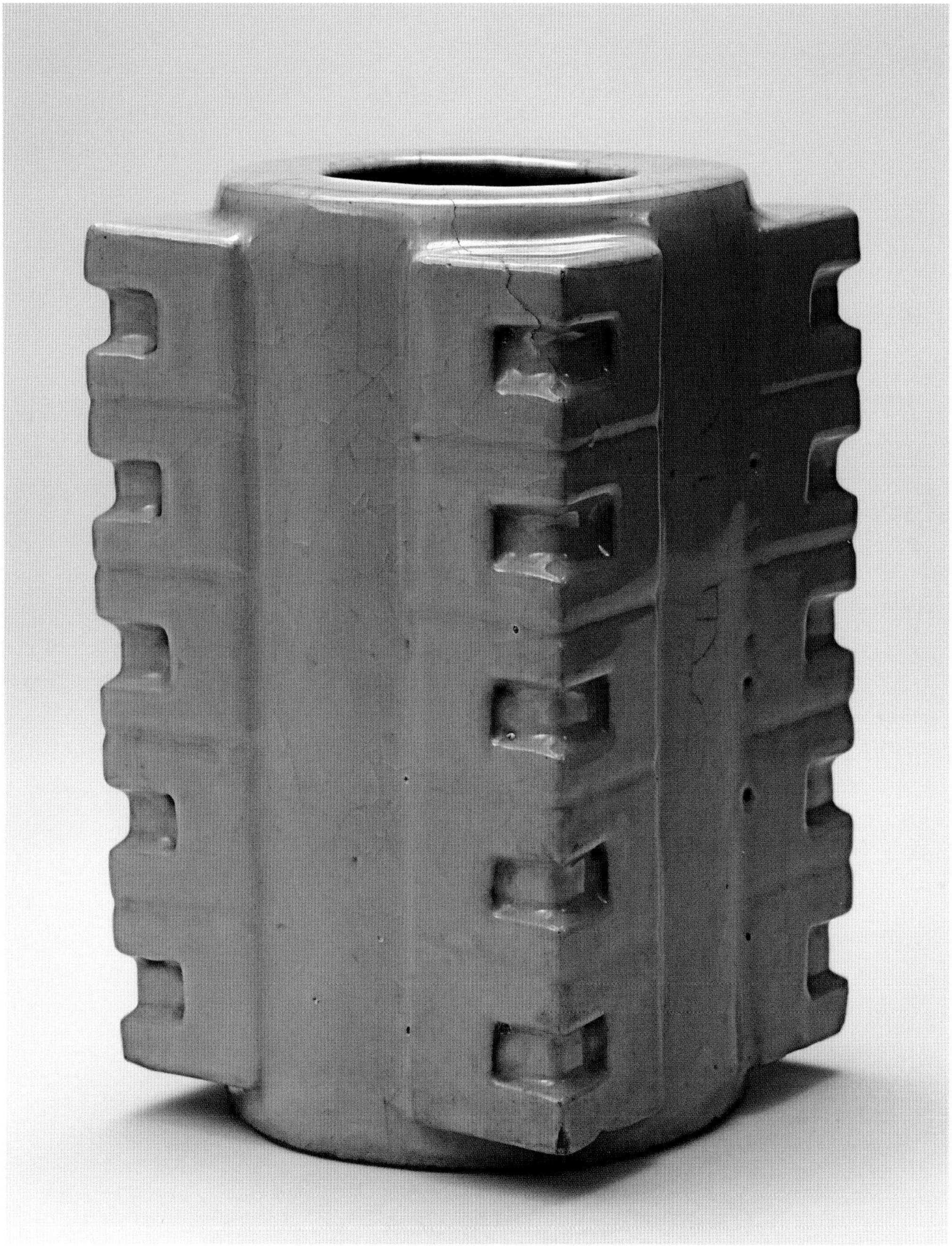

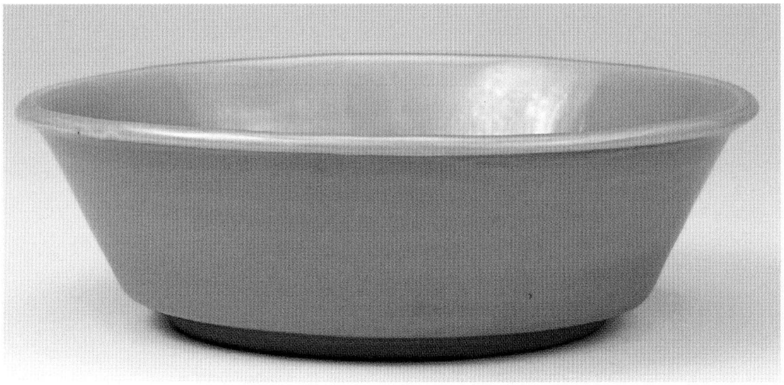

17 Brush-washer with celadon glaze
Longquan ware 龍泉窯
Longquan region, Zhejiang province 浙江省，龍泉地區
Southern Song dynasty, AD 1127–1279
Height 5.3 cm, diameter 17 cm
PDF 284

Archaeologists excavated similar porcelain brush-washers in 1991 in a Southern Song context, in the Jinyucun hoard of Suining city, Sichuan province, but none of this large size. These vessels have an angular profile, with a thickened rolled rim and a low foot and are glazed inside, outside and on the base with a broad-bean-coloured celadon glaze. Some of the most beautiful celadon glazes were made at Longquan in the Southern Song dynasty. The Longquan clay is light grey but reoxidizes during the cooling process in the kiln so that it appears orangey-red where it is unglazed, as is the case here on the foot ring. The Longquan kilns were non-official kilns whose workers nevertheless made ceramics for the imperial household and also for middle-class patrons and foreign customers. Potters at Longquan used locally available clay and glaze materials which ensured that, although they were heavily influenced by production techniques employed at the *guan* kilns, their output was quite different.

18 Pair of funerary urns with celadon glaze
Longquan ware 龍泉窯
Longquan region, Zhejiang province 浙江省，龍泉地區
Southern Song dynasty, AD 1127–1279
PDF 204 a and b

These celadon funerary urns are decorated around the shoulder with two 'animals of the four directions'. On the left, the White Tiger of the West is pursuing a dog and on the right the Green Dragon of the East is chasing a flaming pearl. The birds on the covers may allude to the Red Bird of the South; but the symbol of the north, a tortoise with a snake, is not present. In China, artists decorated coffins and tombs with these creatures from the Han dynasty (206 BC–AD 220) onwards. The sides are decorated with stylized lotus petals that have raised ribs. Excavators have discovered jars of this type at the Dayao [大窯] kiln site in Longquan county, as well as in Southern Song dynasty tombs in the Longquan area. They appear to be part of local southern burial practice, probably used for provisions for the afterlife such as grain, and were neither exported nor made for the court. These vessels are unusual within the Sir Percival David Collection as they are directly connected with interment rather than collected as heirloom pieces.

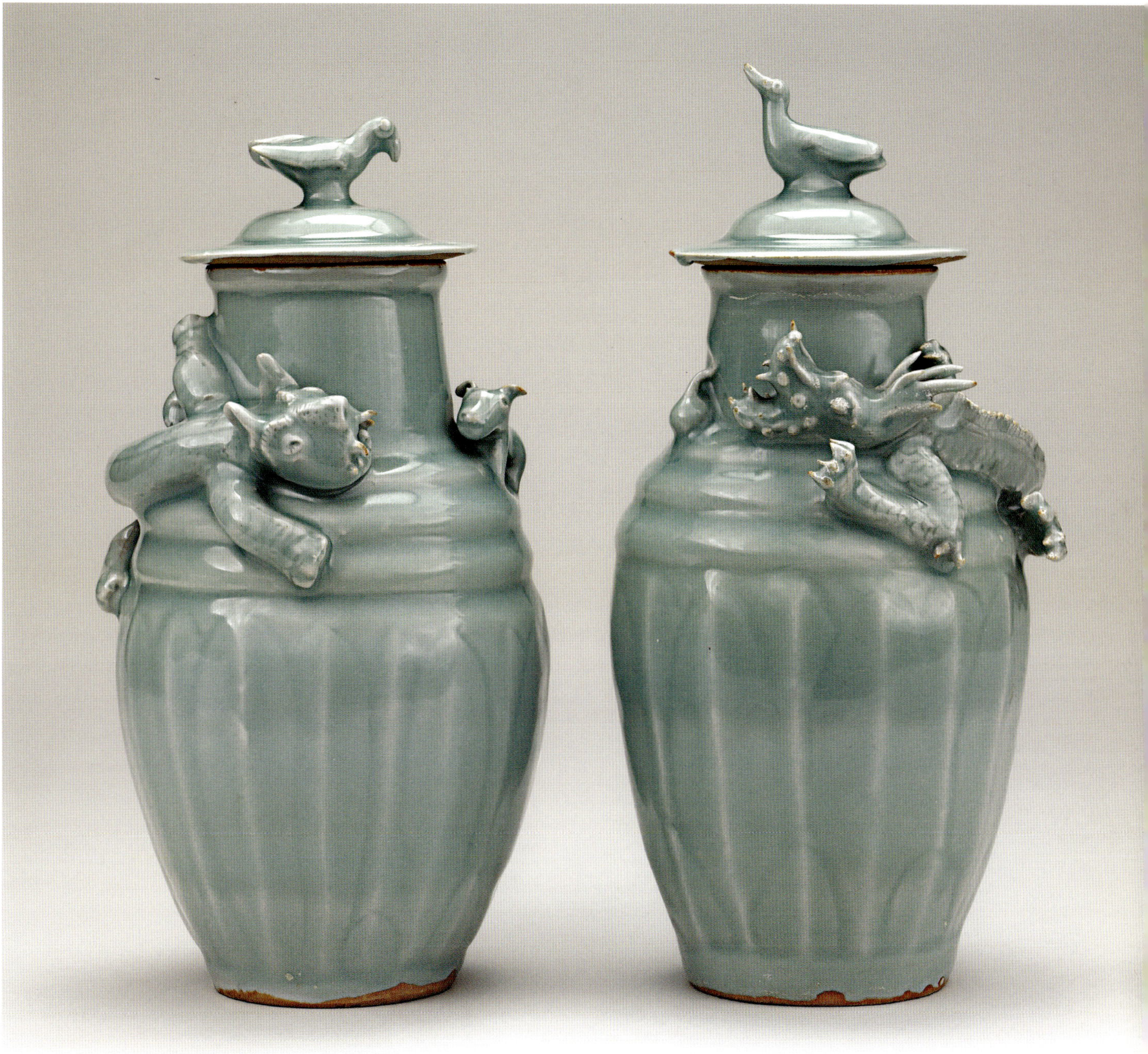

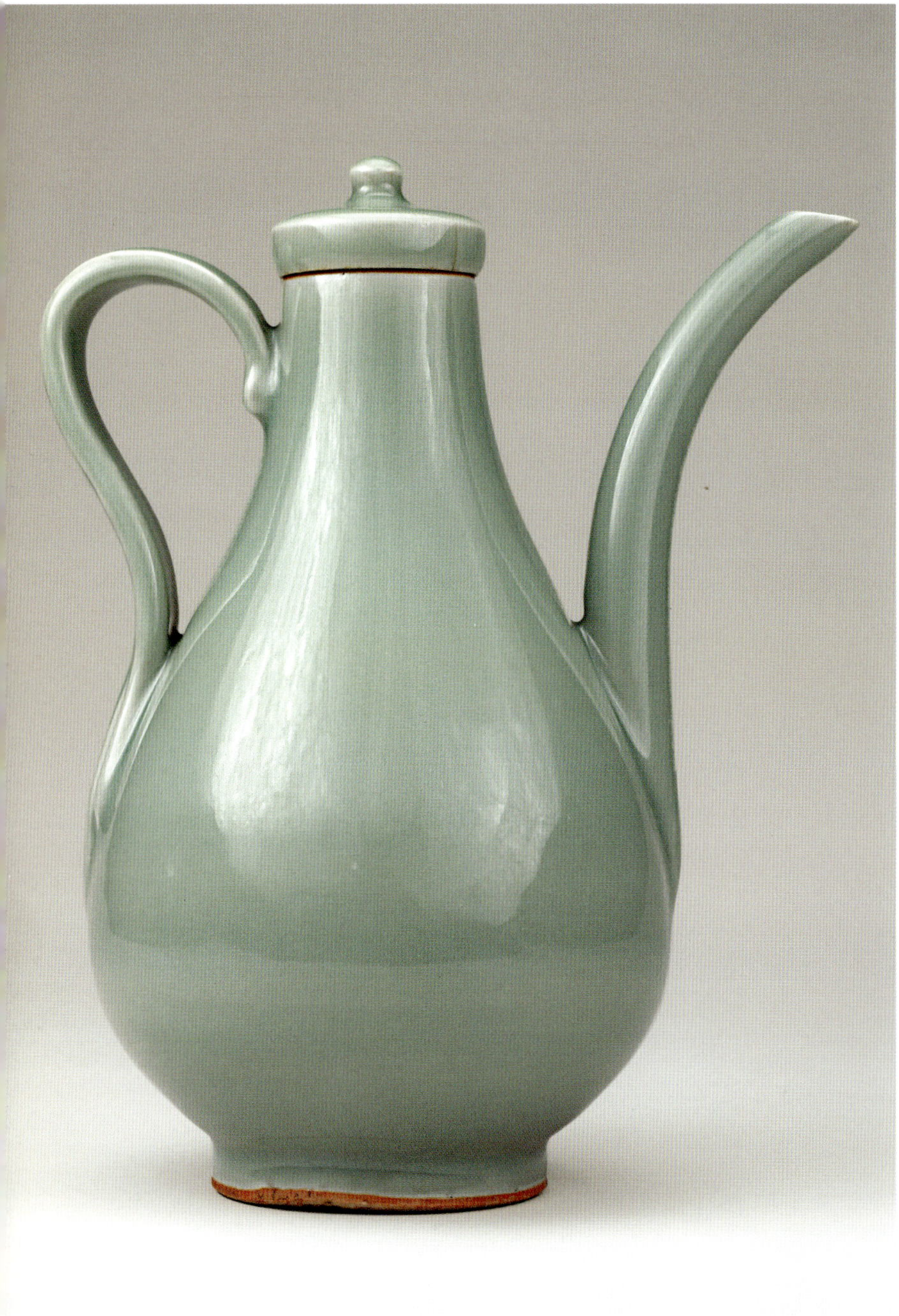

19 Covered ewer with celadon glaze

Longquan ware 龍泉窯

Longquan region, Zhejiang province 浙江省, 龍泉地區

Yuan dynasty, about AD 1300–1368

Height 21.1 cm

PDF 218

This attractive celadon ewer is an outstandingly fine survivor of its type. Potters modelled its elegant pear-shaped body, long slim curved spout, curved handle and domed-knob cover after a metal prototype, probably silverware but possibly bronze. Its detailing, such as the base of the handle that splits into three perfectly formed sections, is very fine. Later, during the reign of the first Ming emperor (AD 1368–98), ewers were crafted at Longquan with pear-shaped bodies but with carved decoration and a curlicue strut attaching the body to the curve of the spout. R.L. Hobson records that this ewer was acquired by Sir Percival David from the Hirooka Collection in Kobe, Japan. Green-glazed wares, known as celadons in English, 青瓷 [*qingci*] in Chinese and 青瓷 [*seiji*] in Japanese, were particularly admired in Japan, where they were regarded as treasures, collected as antiques, and suitable shapes were used for the tea ceremony.

20 Vase with celadon glaze and brown spots

Longquan ware 龍泉窯

Longquan region, Zhejiang province 浙江省, 龍泉地區

Yuan dynasty, about AD 1300–1368

Height 27.2 cm

PDF 217

Potters decorated this vase inside and out with a broad-bean-coloured glaze. They achieved the brown spots by applying iron-rich pigment (such as iron filings) directly on to the celadon glaze in random patches before firing. This decorative technique appears to have enjoyed a relatively short-lived popularity in the Yuan dynasty (AD 1279–1368). The shape of this vase, with its trumpet-like neck and ovoid body, is also an innovation of the Yuan era. Archaeologists recovered a small group of objects with similar iron-brown spots from the cargo of a ship wrecked in the waters near the Dokdo islets off the Shinan coast in southwest Korea, dateable to AD 1323. Of the 17,000 ceramics on board, over half were from Longquan. The ship is believed to have been travelling from Ningbo in southern China to Korea on its way to Japan. Traditionally this type of spotted celadon is known as 飛青磁 [*tobiseiji*, splashed celadon] in Japan and is greatly prized by collectors there.

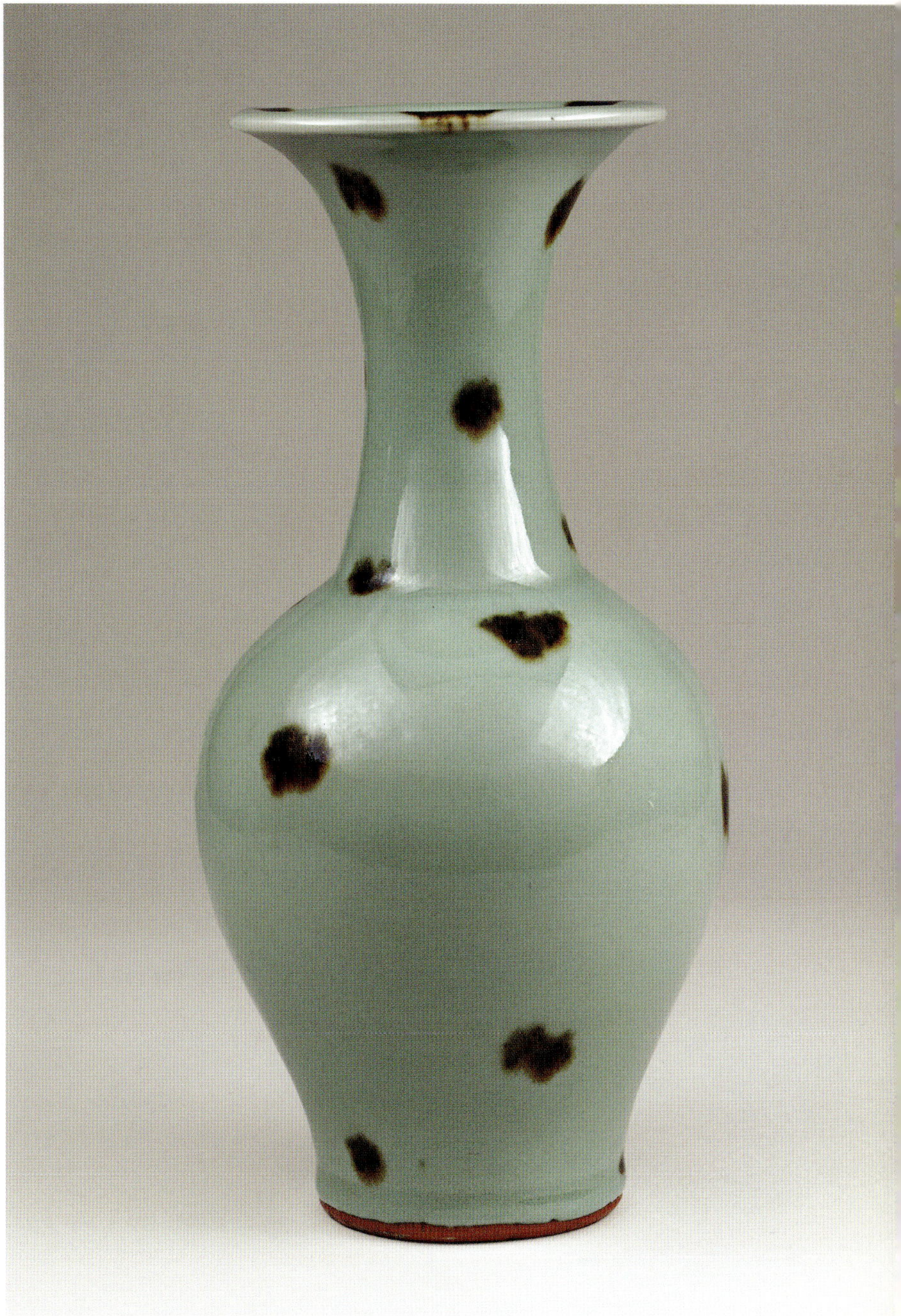

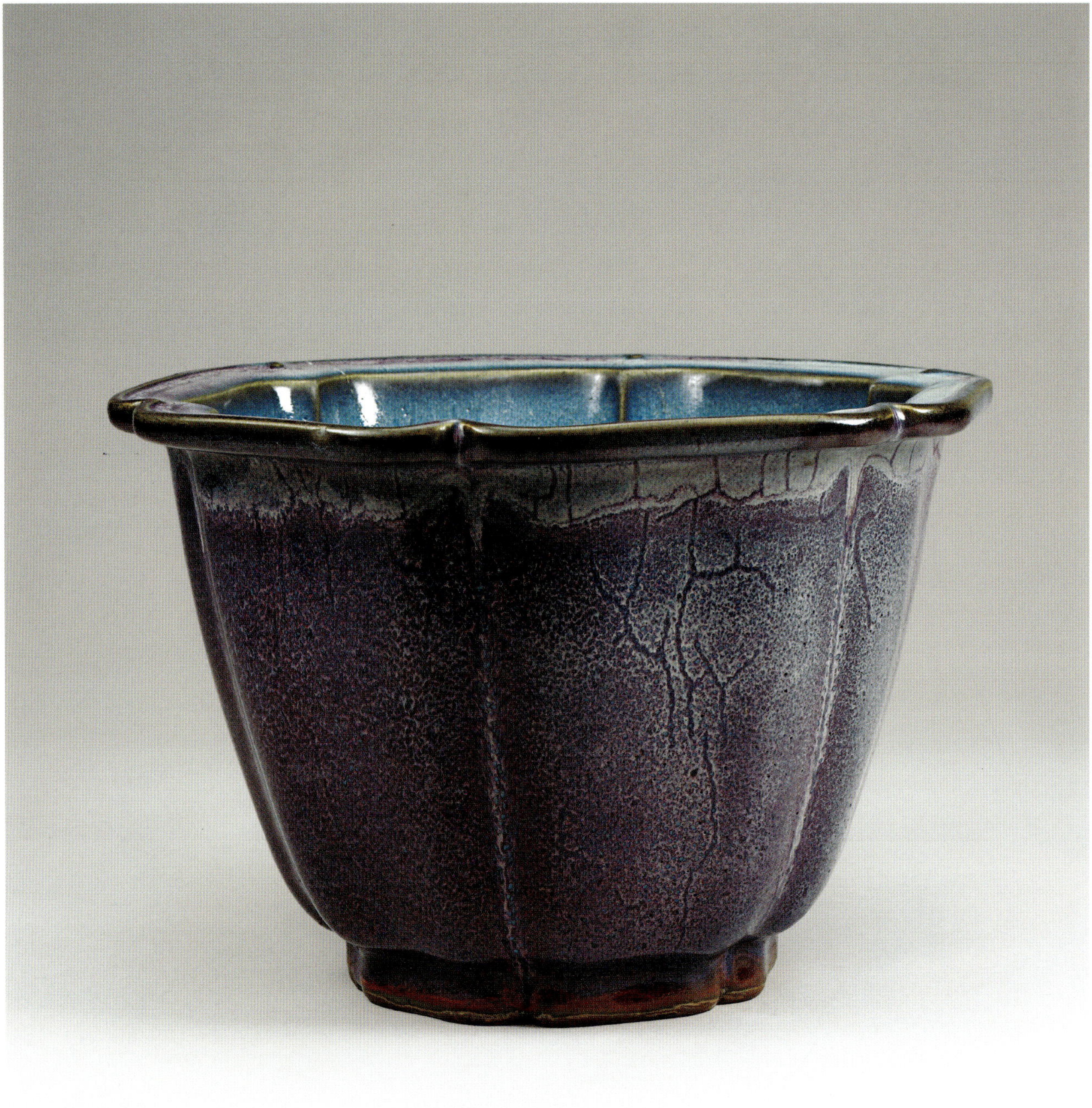

21 Lobed flowerpot
Numbered or Official Jun ware 官鈞窯
Juntai, Yuxian, Henan province 河南省，禹縣，鈞台
Ming dynasty, about AD 1368–1435
Height 17.4 cm; diameter 26.1 cm
PDF A11

If the inscription incised into the base is to be relied on, this flowerpot was used by the Qianlong emperor (ruled AD 1736–95) to decorate the Iris and Orchid Chambers 芝蘭室用 [*zhi lan shi yong*, 'for use in the Iris and Orchid Chambers'] within the 重華宮 [*Zhong hua gong*, 'Palace of Cherished Glory'] of the Forbidden City. This palace was part of the emperor's private quarters. The flowerpot is covered with a glassy, lavender-coloured glaze outside and sky blue inside. It belongs to a type of Jun ware inscribed with numbers and is incised with the character 五 [*wu*], meaning five, on the base. The numbers used on these wares range from one to ten with one the largest in size and ten the smallest. This flowerpot is drilled with five holes for drainage and originally would have rested on a matching six-lobed saucer. Unlike earlier Song, Jin and Yuan Jun wares, numbered Jun wares have not been found in tombs, but are found in the palace collections suggesting they were only made for court use.

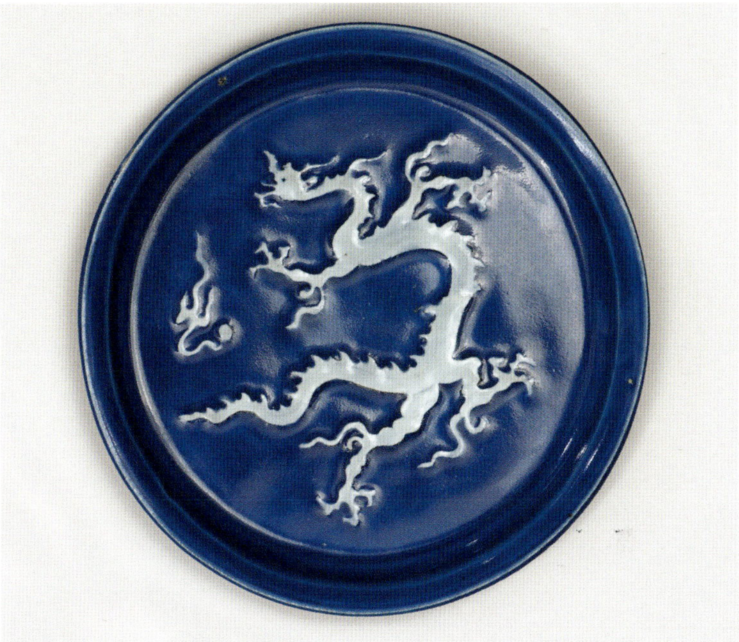

22 Blue dish with a white dragon and flaming pearl
Jingdezhen, Jiangxi province 江西省，景德鎮
Yuan dynasty, about AD 1320–50
Height 1.5 cm; diameter 15.7 cm
PDF A562

This porcelain dish is remarkable for its extremely rare technique of combining a white design with a monochrome blue ground. Potters first applied a cobalt-blue monochrome glaze to all but the base, which was left unglazed. Next they cut out in thin clay a sinewy dragon pursuing a flaming pearl and applied it to the dish. They used slip to add details such as the three claws, incised the dragon's scales, and painted its eyes blue for greater dynamism. Finally they covered it all with a transparent glaze and fired the dish at the high temperature of about 1280–1320°C. Originally the dragon may have been gilded. The flat shape of the dish was probably based on a metal prototype.

23 Wine jar with applied cobalt-blue and copper-red decoration

Jingdezhen, Jiangxi province 江西省，景德鎮
Yuan dynasty, about AD 1320–50
Height 33 cm; diameter 29.5 cm
PDF B661

When originally made in the first half of the fourteenth century, this jar demonstrated the latest ceramic technology by combining underglaze-red and underglaze-blue painted motifs with applied decoration all on one piece. The jar has an ovoid body and short neck with an unglazed base. Porcelain decorators painted the flowers of the four seasons – peony (spring), lotus (summer), chrysanthemum (autumn) and prunus (winter) – in a collar with four ornate *ruyi*-shaped panels around the neck and lappets around the foot. Around the body are four quatrefoil panels showing copper-red flowers, cobalt-blue leaves and rocks in applied relief with incised details. These panels are double-framed by thin cords of clay, scored to suggest beading, which was another feature of Yuan ceramics. The glaze is blue-tinged as a result of the reduction firing and unevenly applied so that it appears in thin and thick streaks around the body.

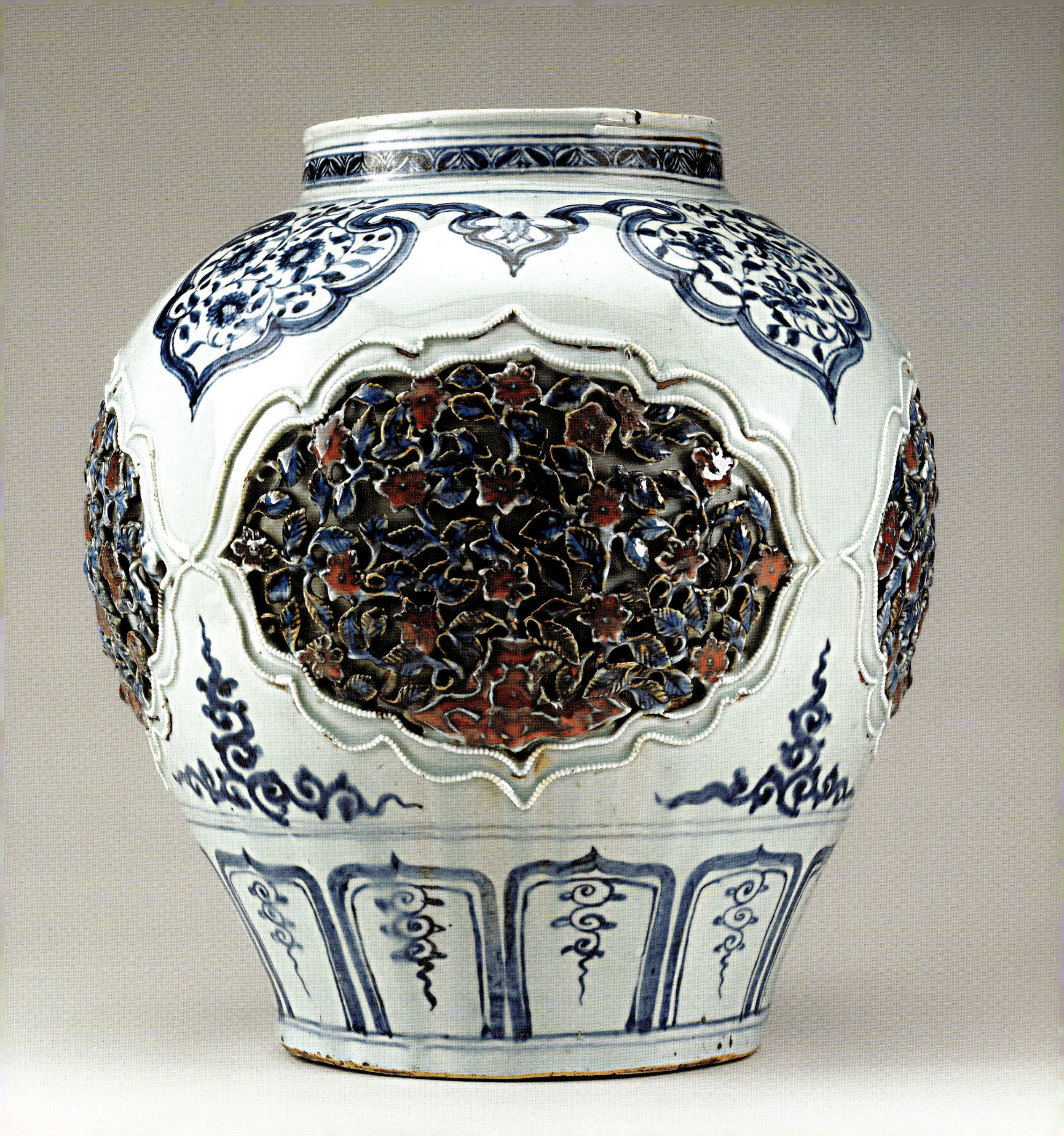

24 Blue-and-white temple vases

Jingdezhen, Jiangxi province 江西省，景德鎮

Yuan dynasty, dated equivalent to AD 1351

Height 63.6 cm

PDF B613 and B614

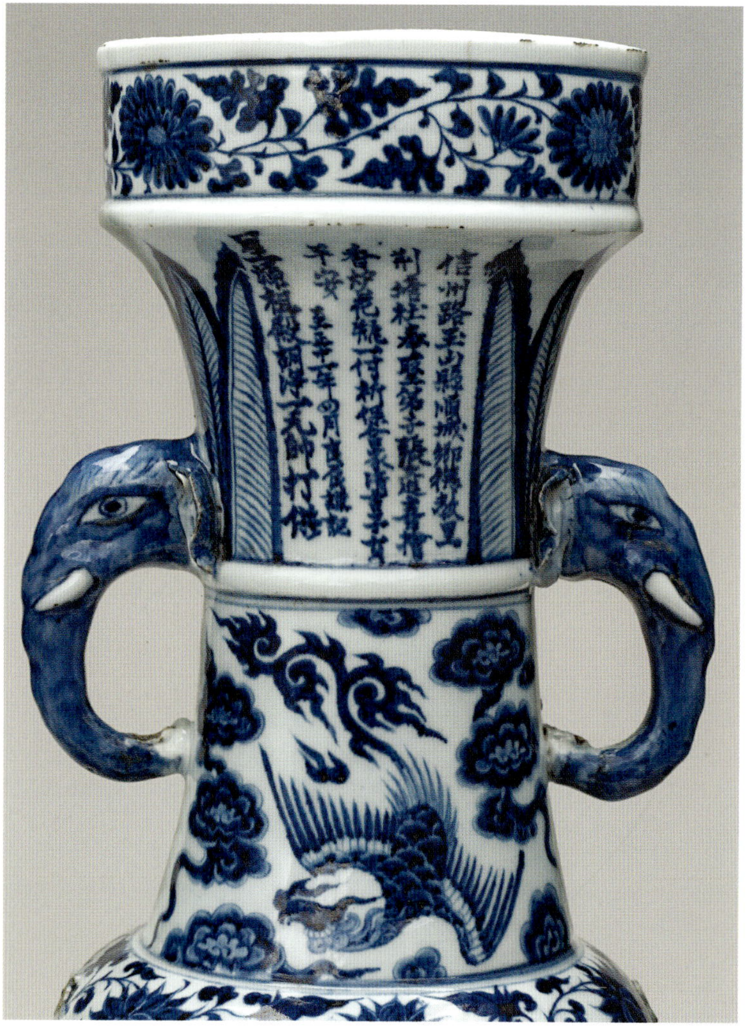

These underglaze-blue painted altar vases, modelled after bronzes, are the best-known porcelains in the Sir Percival David Collection and are among the most famous in the world. They are traditionally called the 'David Vases' by scholars and connoisseurs. Their importance lies in the dated inscriptions on one side of their necks. This long dedication is the earliest known on blue-and-white wares. Indeed no other piece of genuine Yuan blue-and-white porcelain with a dated inscription exists. It records that in AD 1351 a man named Zhang Wenjin from Yushan county [玉山縣] presented these two vases and an incense burner (the whereabouts of which is unknown), to a Daoist temple in Xingyuan 星源 (modern day Wuyuan county 婺源縣). Yushan county is in northeast Jiangxi, which lies 120 km southeast of Jingdezhen, where these vases were made. This inscription provides unique documentary evidence for studying the development of blue-and-white wares and demonstrates that their production was already well established at Jingdezhen by AD 1351. Originally the vases would have had porcelain rings attached through the elephant-head-shaped handles. In contrast to the West, in China dragons are traditionally considered to be auspicious. They are regarded as controllers of the water supply and ultimately came to symbolize imperial authority.

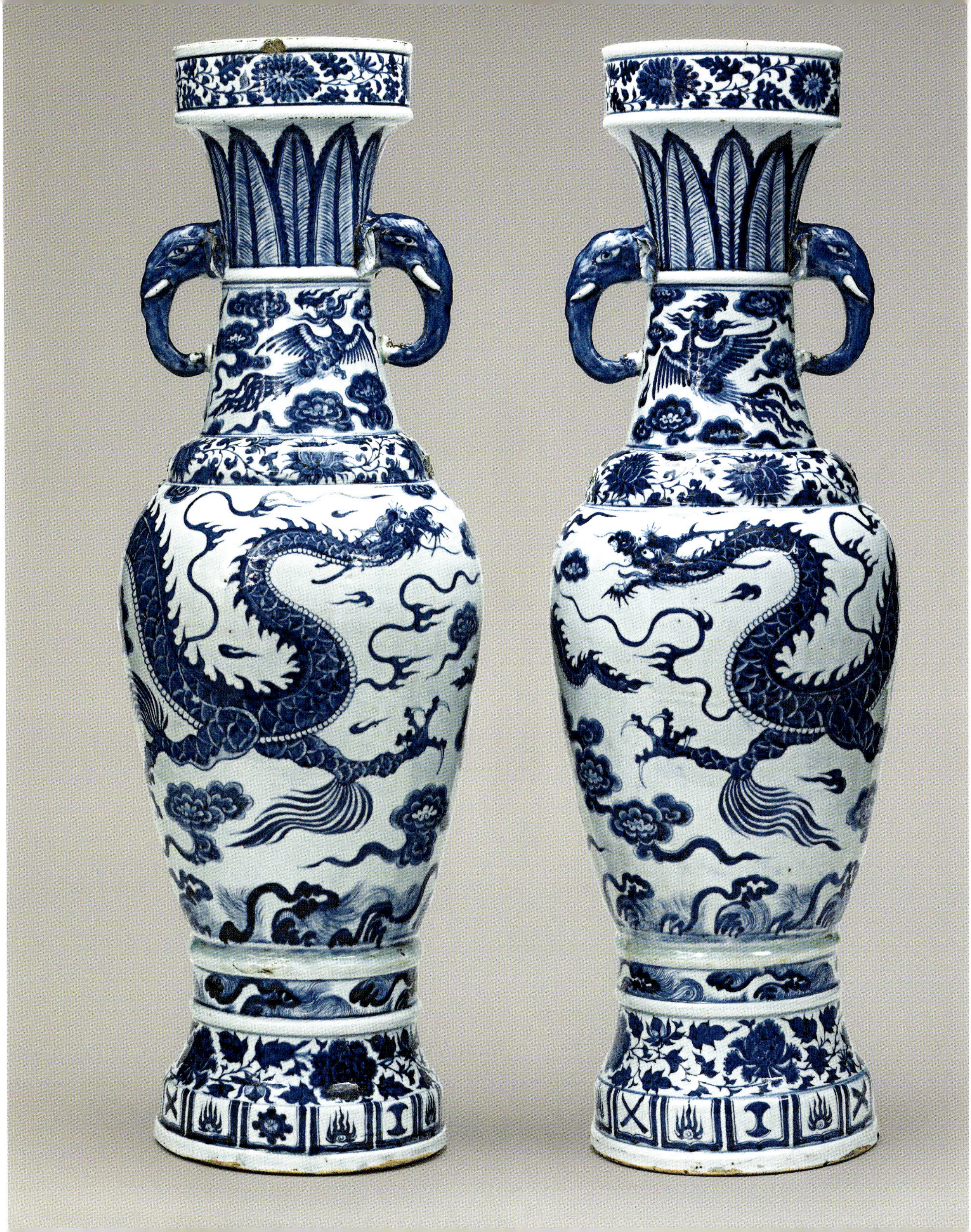

25 Ewer painted in underglaze red
Jingdezhen, Jiangxi province 江西省，景德鎮
Ming dynasty, Hongwu period, AD 1368–98
Height 32.5 cm; width 25.2 cm
PDF A696

Copper-oxide pigment, used to create underglaze-red designs, is extremely difficult to fire successfully at the high temperatures required for porcelain production. The pigment is more volatile and harder to fire effectively than cobalt oxide, which was used to create blue-and-white designs. If the process was successful, as here, copper oxide could fire bright red but if not, it fired pale, liverish red, grey or almost black. Potters made far greater quantities of monochrome red and underglaze-red wares in the Hongwu period (AD 1368–98) than in the Yuan dynasty (AD 1279–1368). Whereas in the Yuan dynasty they were experimental wares, in the Ming dynasty they were produced on a larger scale but remained rare. Originally this ewer had a domed porcelain cover with a lotus bud finial and a loop to marry up with the ring on top of the handle. Details such as the fine raised vertical rib down the handle and the three studs at its base refer to the metalwork version, of which the porcelain is a copy. Archaeologists excavated similar ewers with underglaze-blue decoration at Dongmentou, Zhushan in Jingdezhen in 1994.

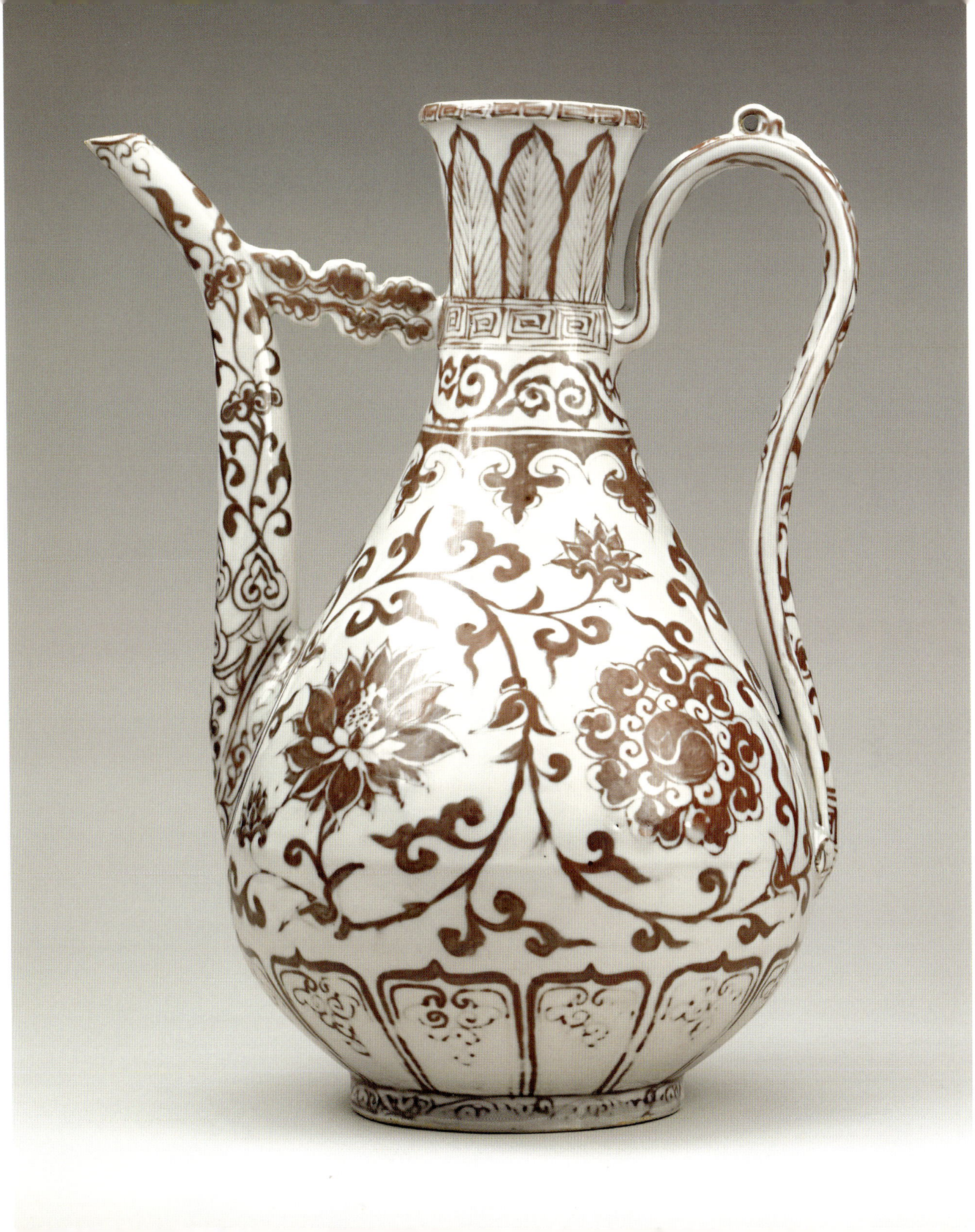

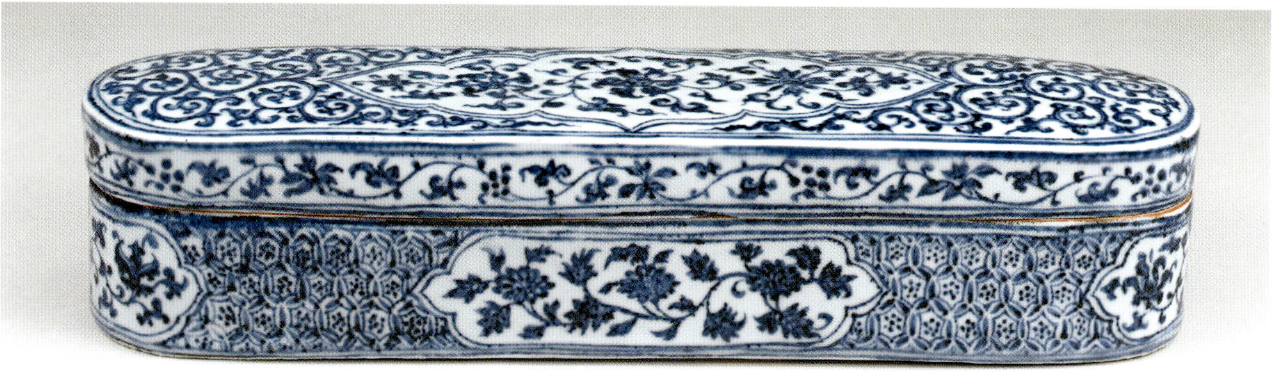

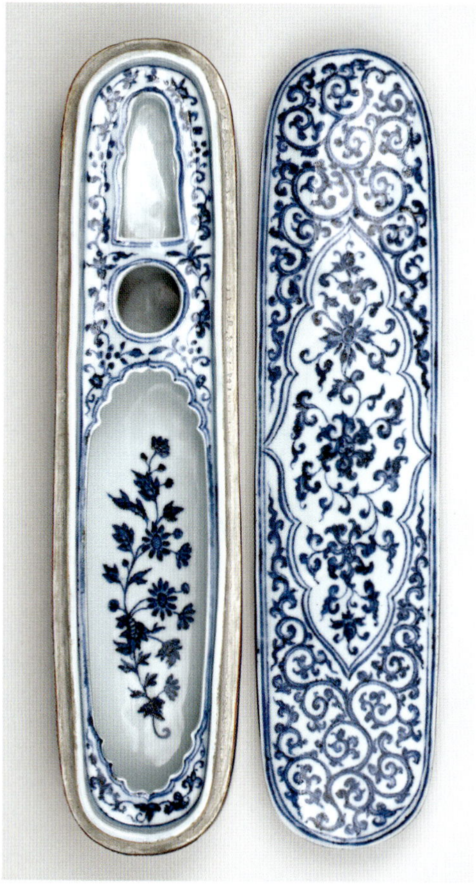

26 Blue-and-white writing box

Jingdezhen, Jiangxi province 江西省，景德鎮
Ming dynasty, Yongle period, AD 1403–24
Height 7.2 cm; width 32 cm; depth 7.8 cm
PDF A629

This writing box has three separate compartments inside, possibly for pens, water or ink, and a well for storing blotting threads. The inside of the cover is painted with the 'Three Friends of Winter' (see no. 43). A box of the same shape but with a different design was excavated from the Yongle strata at the imperial kiln site at Jingdezhen in 1984. The Yongle emperor sponsored trade and exploratory missions abroad. Admiral Zheng He (AD 1371–1433) began his voyages to Southeast Asia, the Near East and Africa under the Yongle emperor's patronage. At court a fashion for exotic Near Eastern-inspired object forms and decorative motifs prevailed. The shape of this writing box as well as its dense decoration is inspired by earlier inlaid metalwork from the Near East as evidenced by brass writing boxes, some inlaid with silver, made in for example Egypt or Syria.

27 Blue-and-white pilgrim flask

Jingdezhen, Jiangxi province 江西省, 景德鎮

Ming dynasty, Yongle period, AD 1403–24

Height 24.2 cm; width 19.8 cm; depth 10.2 cm

PDF B696

This flask is unusual in both its form and decoration. It has a round flattened body with a raised boss on either side, a splayed circular foot, two handles and a globular neck. The decoration is arranged in concentric bands, radiating out from a six-pointed star panel containing a lotus flower, encircled by its own foliage. The dense pattern of decoration is reminiscent of Near Eastern inlaid metalwork. As well as producing objects following the shapes of Near Eastern dining utensils for the overseas market, Jingdezhen craftsmen made objects inspired by Near Eastern forms to fulfil court demands for foreign 'exotica'. Later potters made copies of this type of vessel for the Yongzheng emperor (ruled AD 1723–35), as evidenced by an example in the Palace Museum, Beijing.

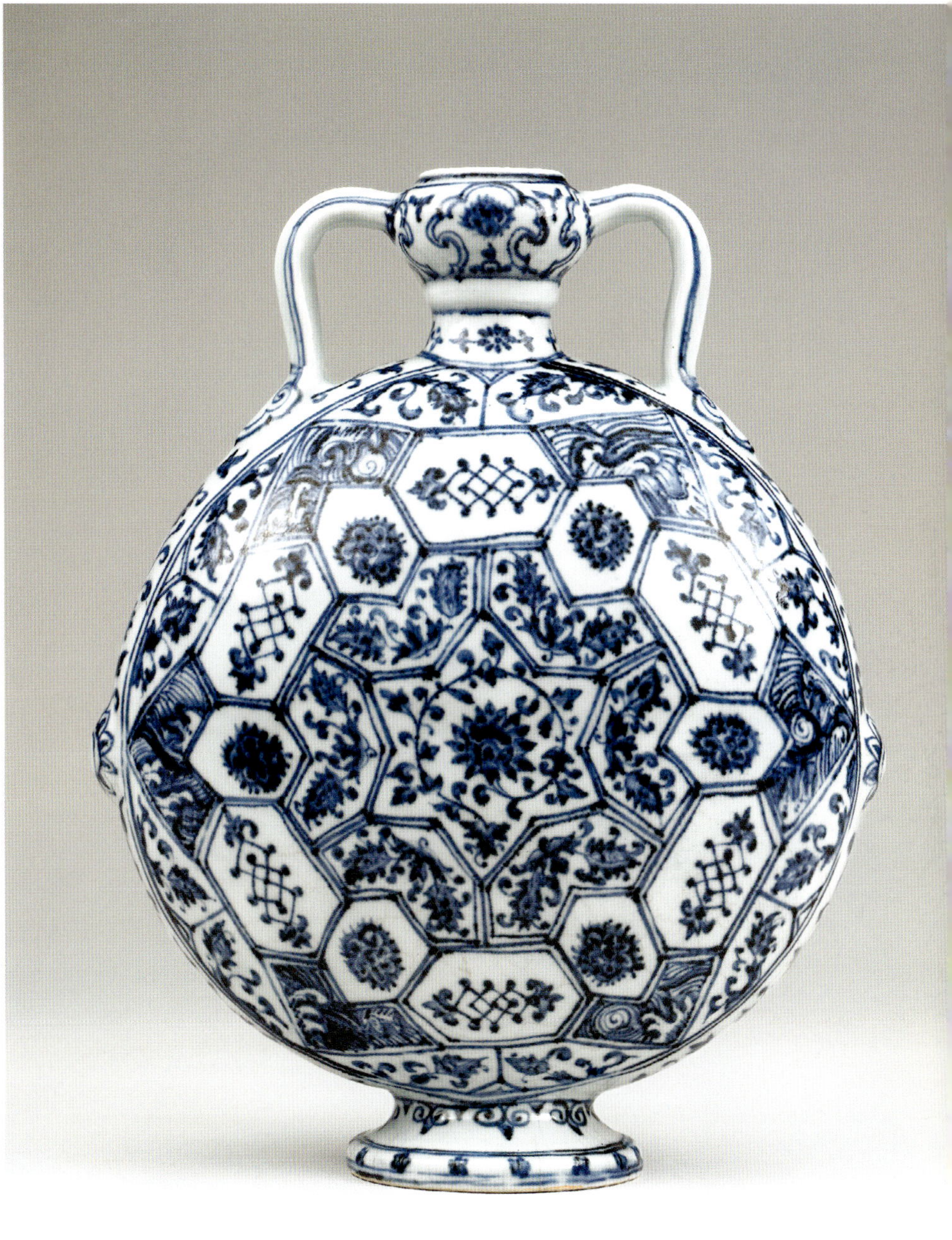

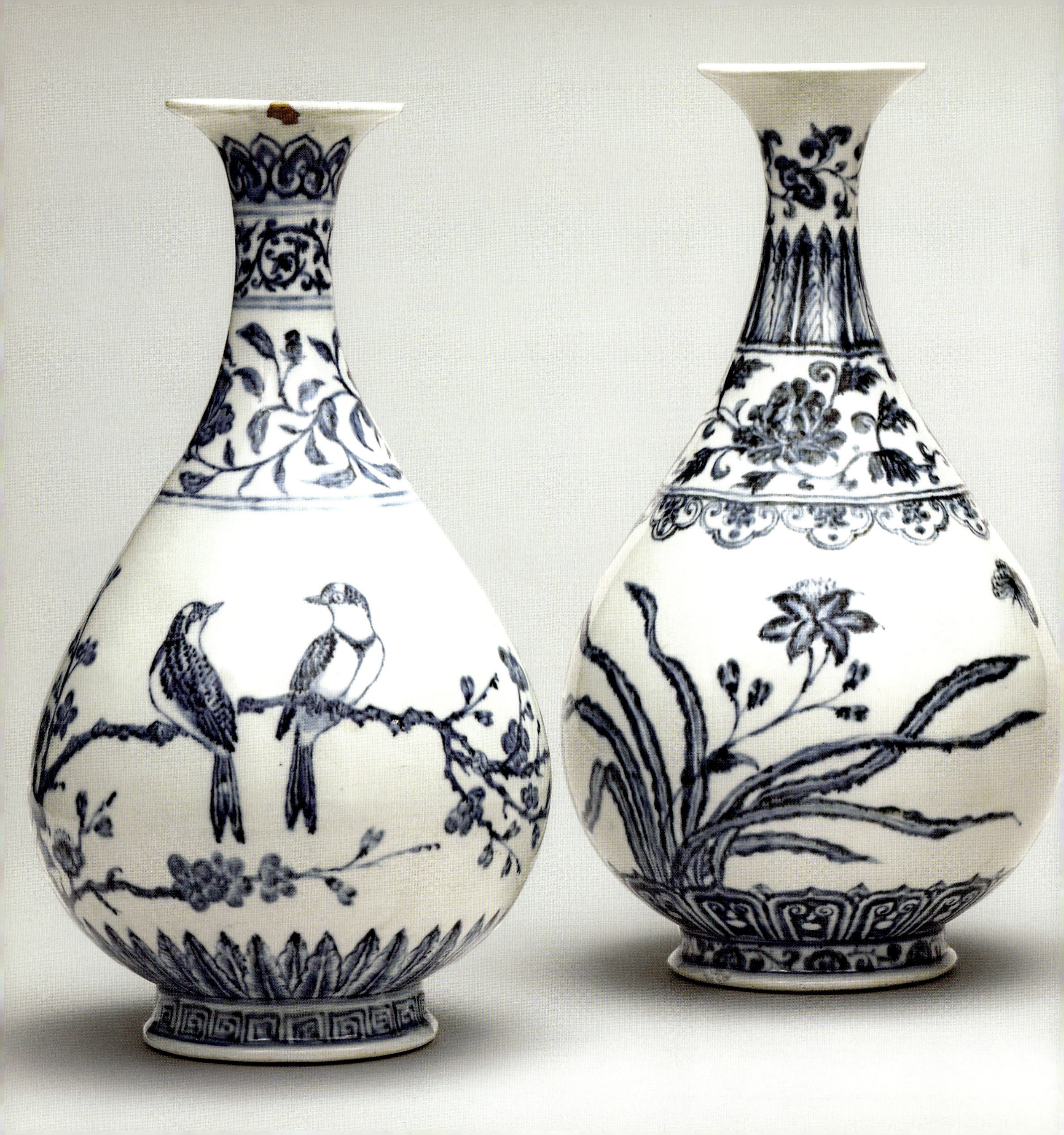

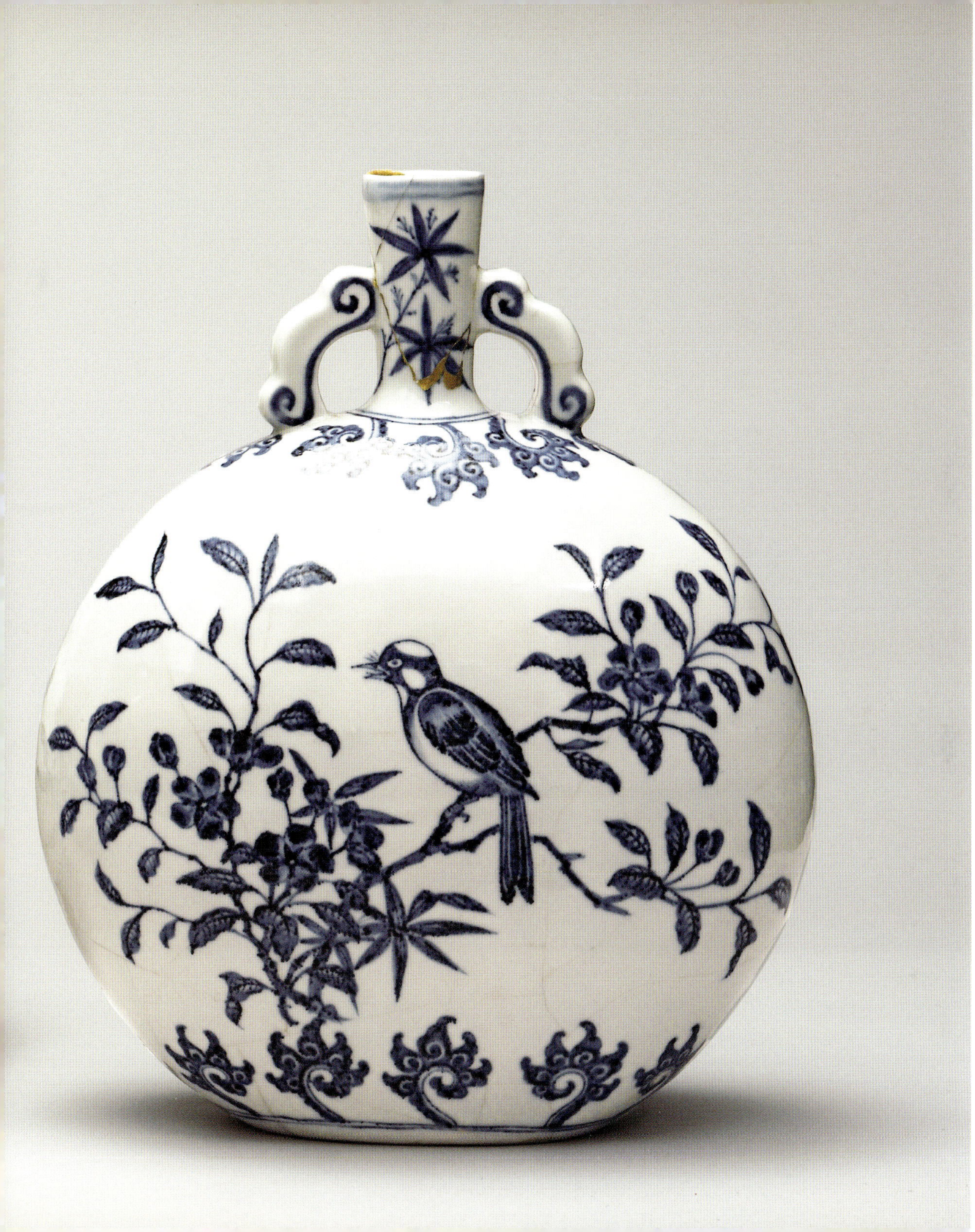

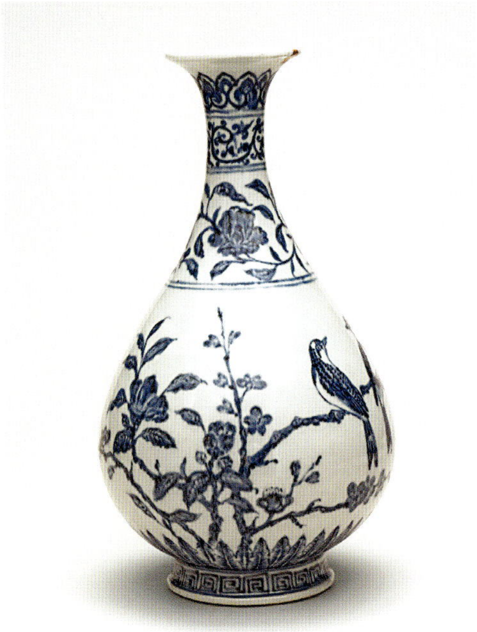

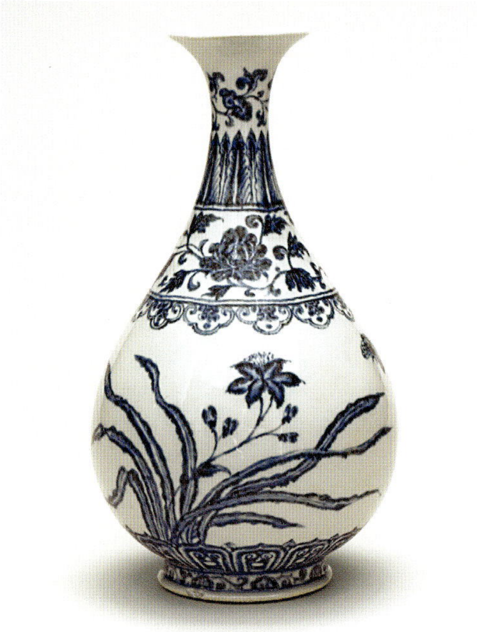

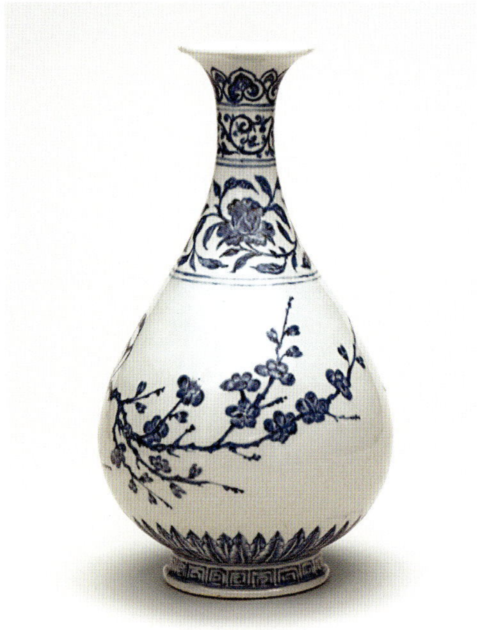

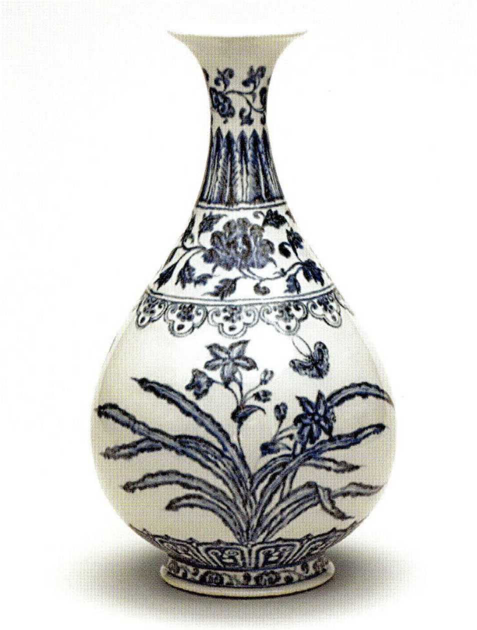

28 Two bottles and a flask with bird and flower designs

Jingdezhen, Jiangxi province 江西省，景德鎮
Ming dynasty, Yongle period, AD 1403–24
Heights 33.5, 34 and 30.8 cm
PDF A614, 601 and A612

Yuan dynasty and Hongwu period blue-and-white wares have dense and crowded decoration. Then, in the Yongle era, potters developed innovative designs that showed off the newly improved quality of the porcelain body, creating a bold contrast between the strong, pure blue designs and a slightly blue-tinged but mostly white ground. In the Yongle reign, potters at Jingdezhen made what many consider to be the finest blue-and-white porcelains ever achieved. These have a lustrous quality never before accomplished and, despite numerous attempts, never successfully imitated. Craftsmen used imported cobalt that fired unevenly, giving shades of blue ranging from pale blue to almost black. The finest-quality designs, such as on these porcelains, were inspired by contemporary fifteenth-century court painting styles, especially as seen in such intimate painting formats as fans and album leaves.

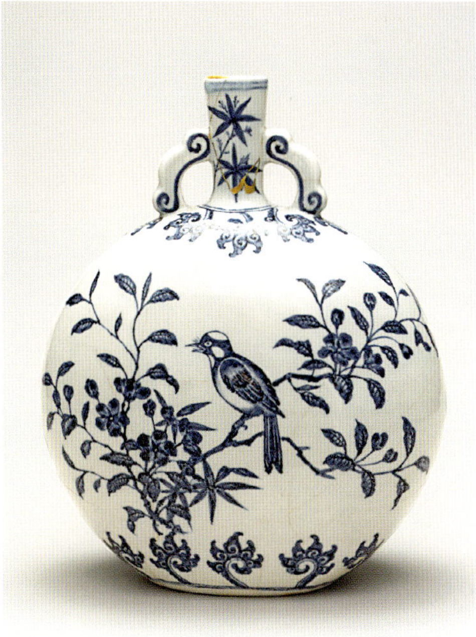

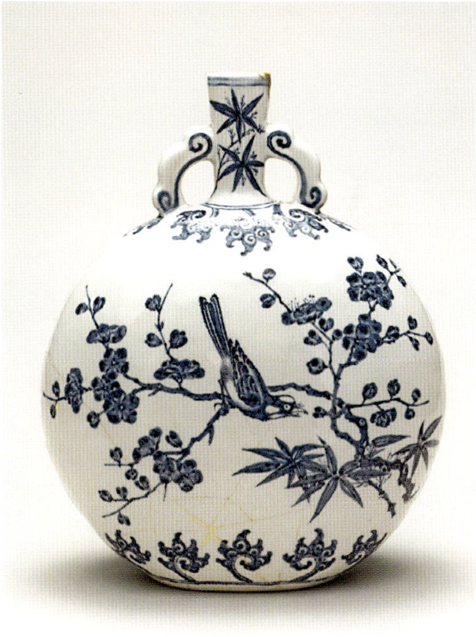

29 Two flasks with dragons

Jingdezhen, Jiangxi province 江西省，景德鎮
Ming dynasty, Yongle period, AD 1403–24
Heights 47.8 and 44.6 cm
PDF B667 and 662

The forms of these flasks are not originally Chinese but are inspired by a Near Eastern shape, possibly of enamelled glass vessels. During both the Yongle (AD 1403–24) and Xuande (AD 1426–35) emperors' reigns, flasks in this large, heavy, bulbous form with variations to the decoration were made at the imperial kilns at Zhushan in Jingdezhen. A flask identical to the one on the right showing a three-clawed dragon with incised details on a wave ground was excavated in 1994 at Dongmentou, Zhushan, Jingdezhen, from the Yongle strata. Such flasks were probably made for court use, possibly as wine decanters, and as trade goods for the Near East as evidenced by similar flasks in the Topkapi Saray Museum in Turkey and in the Ardabil Shrine collection in Iran. During the Yongle emperor's reign, an extraordinary number of men from Jiangxi were employed within the government, which may have contributed to the maintenance of Jingdezhen as the main source of court ceramics.

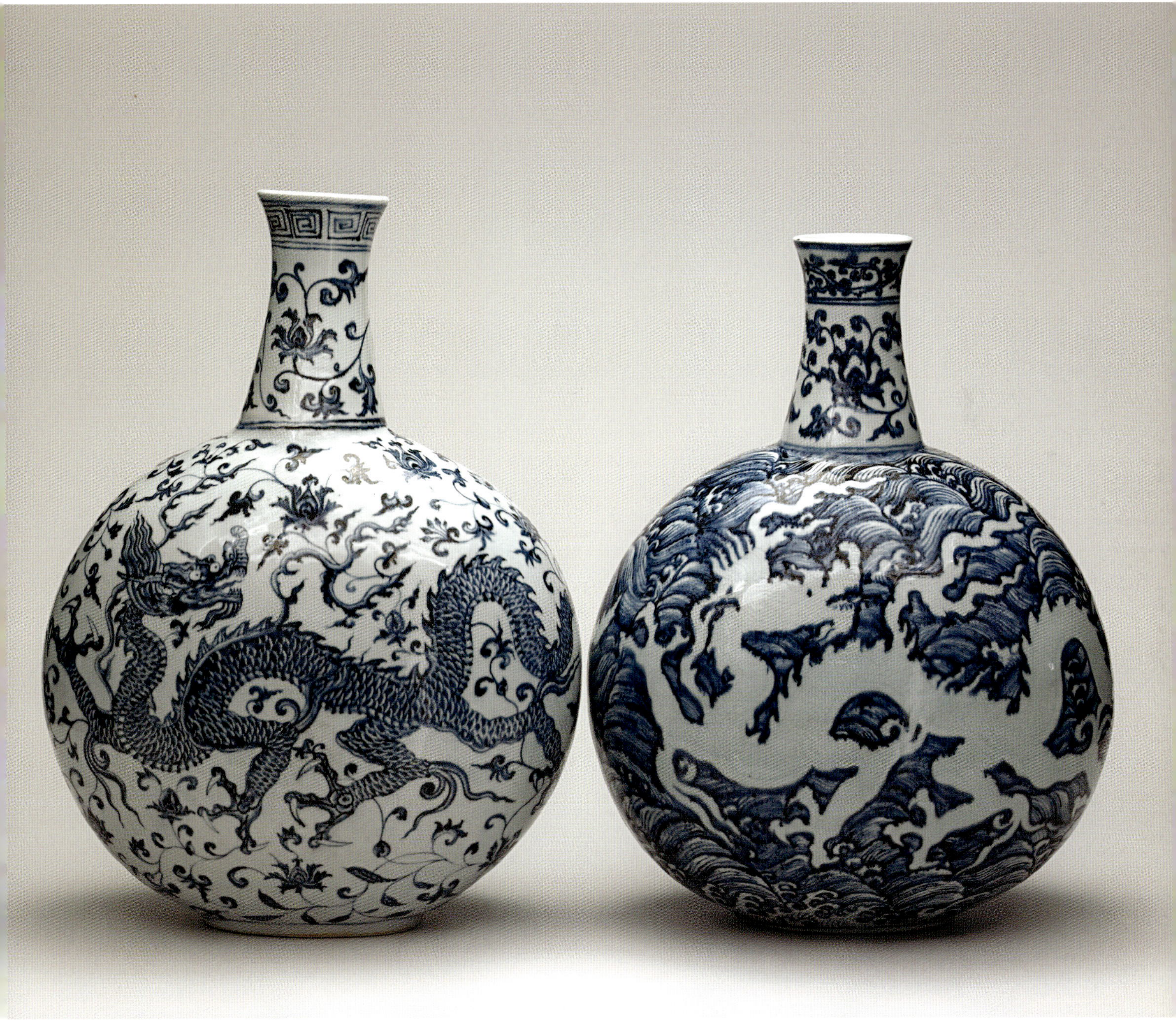

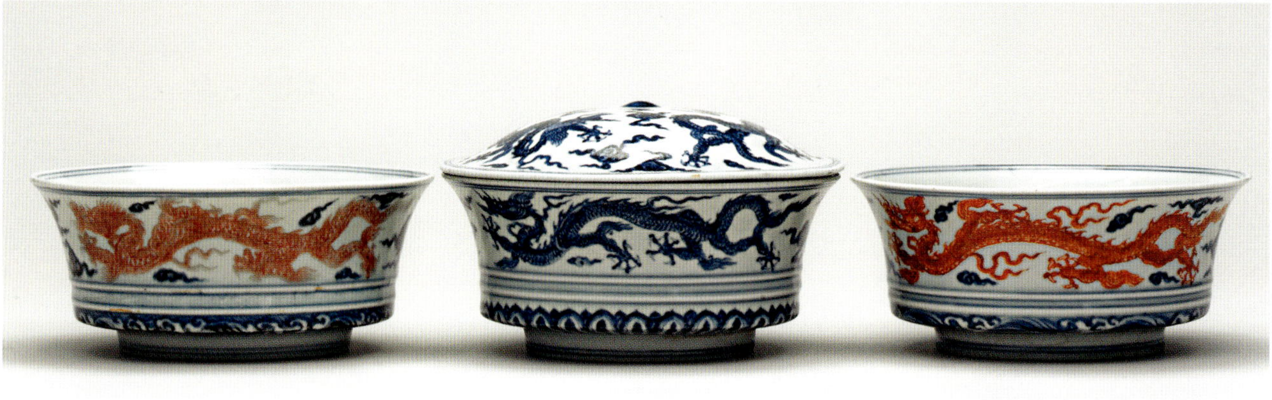

30 Three dragon-decorated bowls
Jingdezhen, Jiangxi province 江西省，景德鎮
Ming dynasty, Xuande mark and period, AD 1426–35
Heights 7.5, 10.3 and 7.5 cm; diameters 17.3, 17.5 and 17.3 cm
PDF A678, 684 and A778

The shape of these bowls with their angular profiles was invented in the Xuande era. Porcelain decorators painted them with a dragon on both sides chasing a flaming pearl among clouds using three different techniques: underglaze copper red, underglaze cobalt blue and overglaze iron red respectively. Porcelain decorators in the early fifteenth century very rarely used iron red. Originally all the bowls would have had matching shallow slightly domed covers and looked like boxes. All three bowls are marked inside with a six-character Xuande reign mark in a double ring. Although in the previous Yongle period a four-character reign mark was sometimes used, the development of what became the standardized six-character reign mark began in the Xuande era as the result of direct official supervision and control of the imperial kilns by the court.

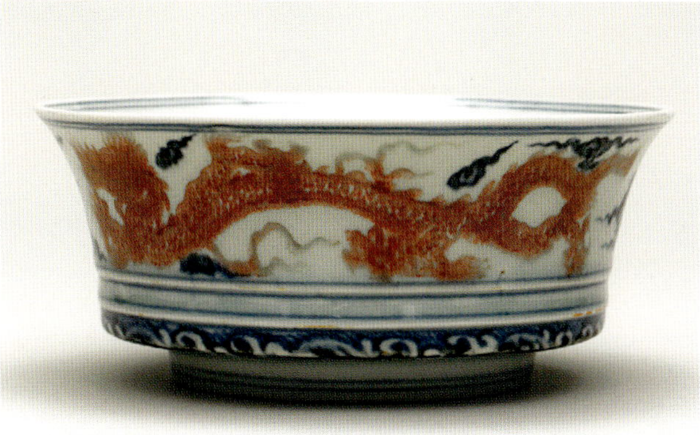
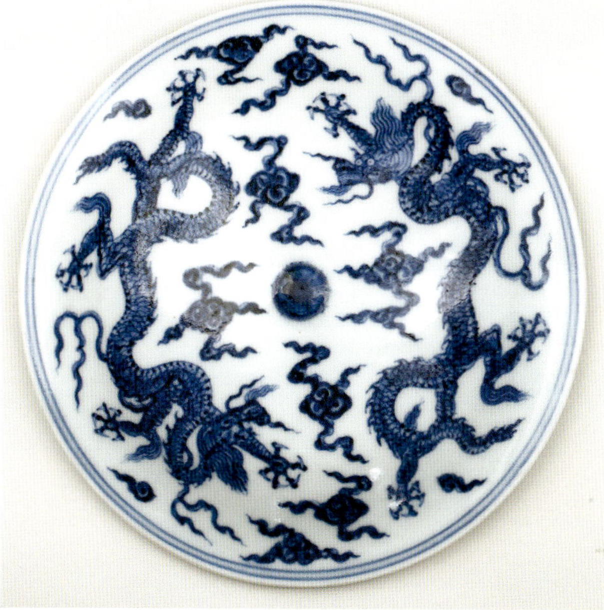
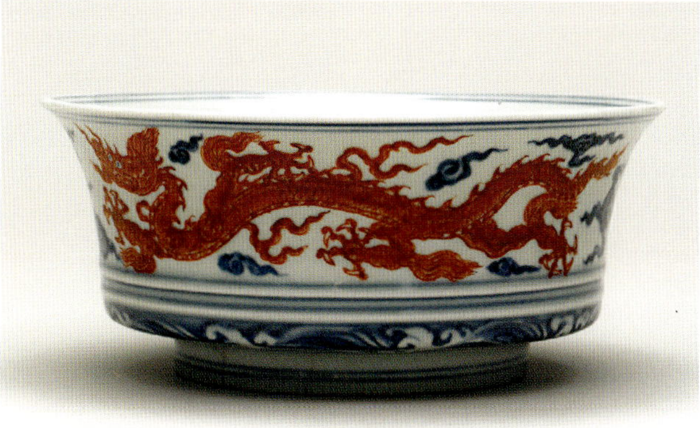
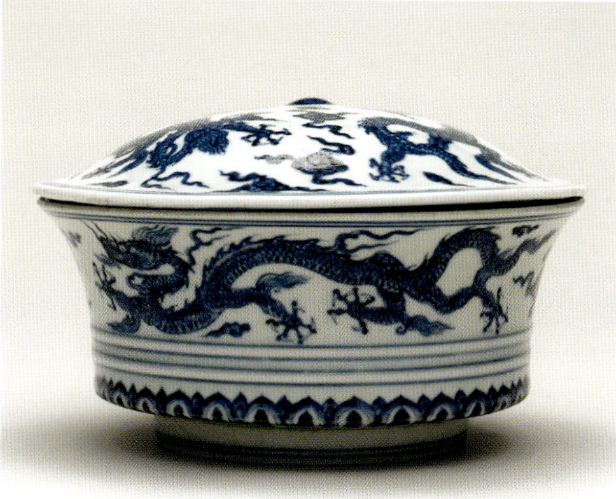

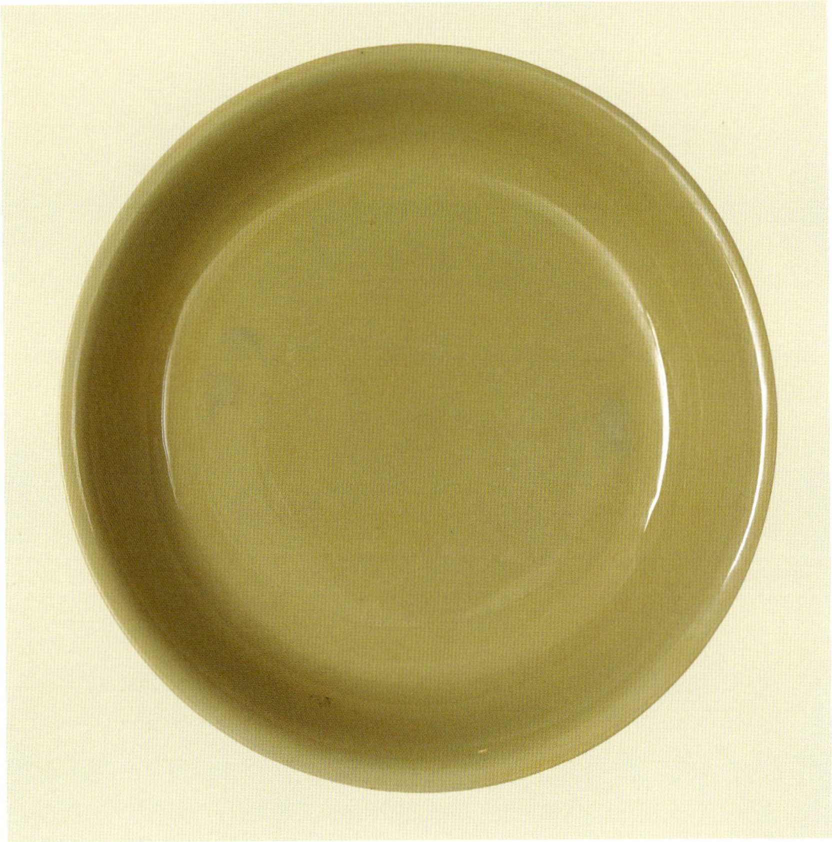

31 Saucer-dish with yellow glaze
Jingdezhen, Jiangxi province 江西省，景德鎮
Ming dynasty, Yongle period, AD 1403–24
PDF 544

Potters of this period were far more innovative than potters of previous eras, as evidenced by the wider range of shapes, decorative techniques and designs excavated from the Yongle imperial kiln site at Jingdezhen. This dish is extraordinarily rare. It demonstrates the first ever use of a monochrome yellow glaze at Jingdezhen. Thereafter this colour glaze was used to decorate court porcelain for the remaining five hundred years of the imperial era in China. Possibly due to technical difficulties or arguably due to taste, very few plain yellow dishes were ever made in the early fifteenth century and fewer survive today. Potters fired the dish twice, first at a porcelain temperature of around 1280–1320°C and then in a second, lower-temperature firing to vitrify the lead-fluxed, iron-pigmented glaze on the inside and outside walls. The base is thinly glazed and reveals a typical early fifteenth-century body.

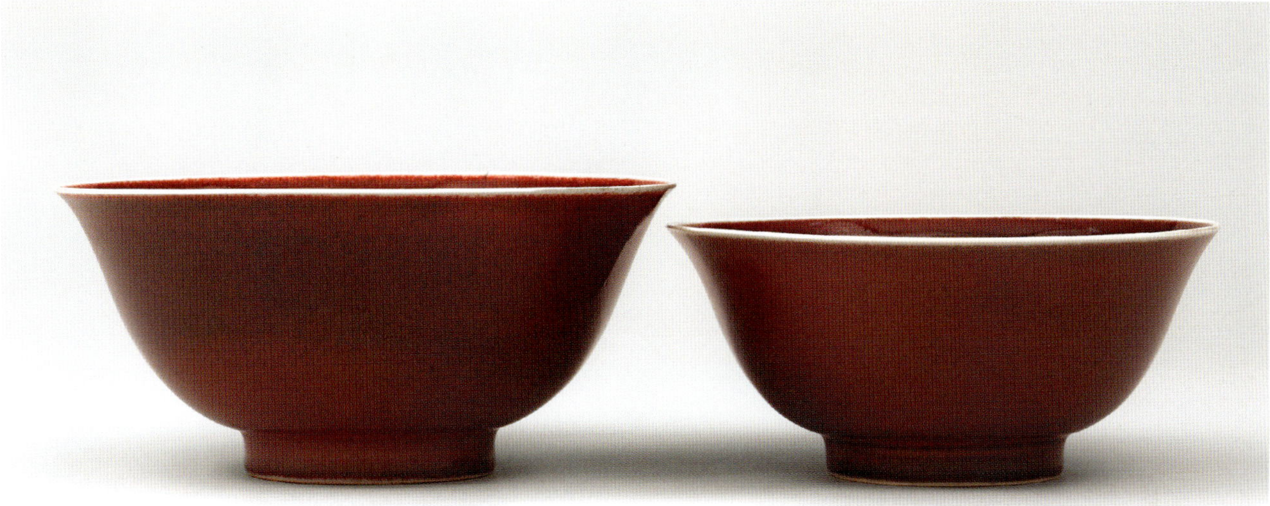

32 Two bowls with copper-red glaze
Jingdezhen, Jiangxi province 江西省，景德鎮
Ming dynasty, Yongle period, AD 1403–24; Xuande mark and period, AD 1426–35
Heights 9.7 and 8.2 cm; diameters 20.7 and 18.7 cm
PDF 585 and A529

'Sacrificial', fresh or deep red monochrome-glazed porcelain of the Yongle and Xuande eras represents the peak of technical achievement at Jingdezhen. As vessels ordered for ritual use by the early fifteenth-century Ming emperors, they enjoy a status above that of other porcelains. The skills used to create these extraordinary red glazes were lost in China from the mid fifteenth century until rediscovered in the late seventeenth and early eighteenth centuries. The glaze has 'crept' at the rims of the bowls to reveal the pure whiteness of the porcelain body. The slightly larger Yongle example has incised stylized lotus lappets around the foot ring rather like the Hongwu monochrome red bowls, whereas the Xuande example is plain. The glassy glaze is covered in tiny pinprick holes like skin pores and the colour possesses an incredible powdery depth, yielding layer upon layer of strong red shades of colour.

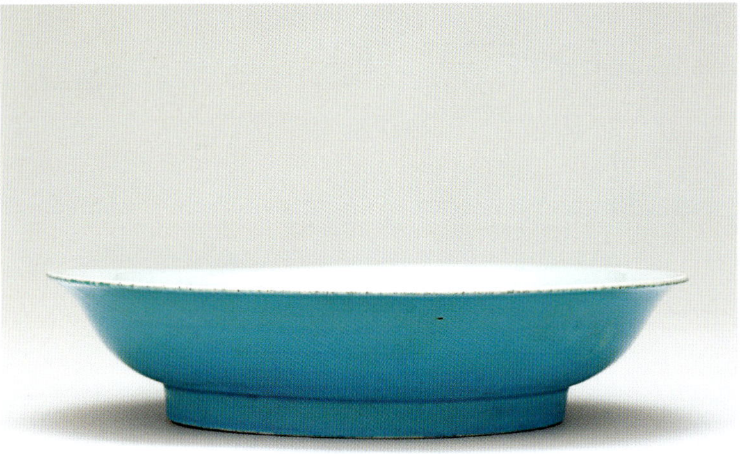

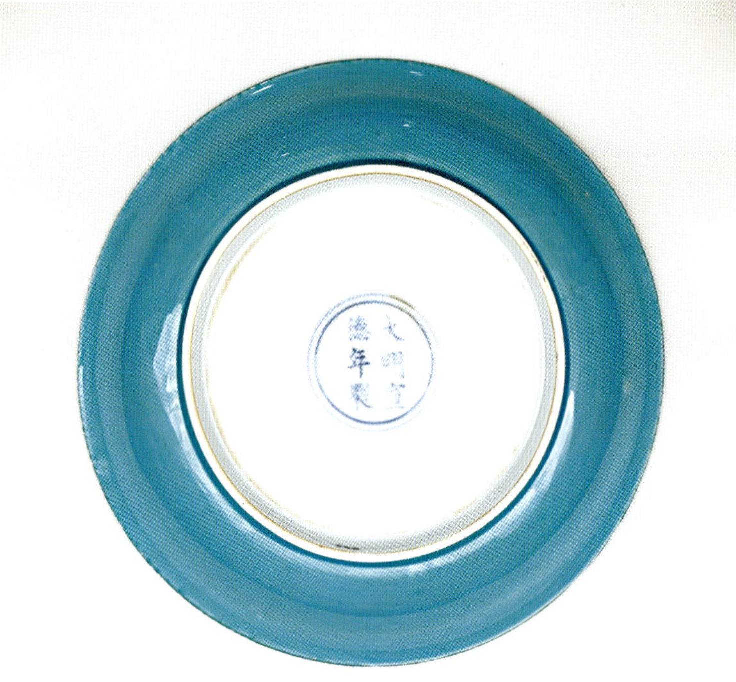

33 Saucer-dish with *anhua* dragons and turquoise glaze

Jingdezhen, Jiangxi province 江西省，景德鎮
Ming dynasty, Xuande mark and period, AD 1426–35
Height 3.4 cm; diameter 18 cm
PDF 550

Craftsmen made this technically accomplished saucer-dish by firing it twice. First they added 暗花 [*anhua*, 'secret or hidden decoration'] of raised slip showing two five-clawed dragons chasing each other and their flaming pearls in the interior walls and incised three auspicious clouds in the centre into the leather-hard clay. Then they painted a six-character reign mark on the base in underglaze blue and coated the whole dish with a clear glaze. Potters fired the dish at a high temperature. Next, workers applied a low-temperature turquoise glaze using a brush on the outside of the dish and refired it at a lower temperature to fix the glaze colour. Archaeologists have excavated dishes of this type at the imperial factory at Zhushan, Jingdezhen. *Anhua* designs can only be properly appreciated when viewed against the light.

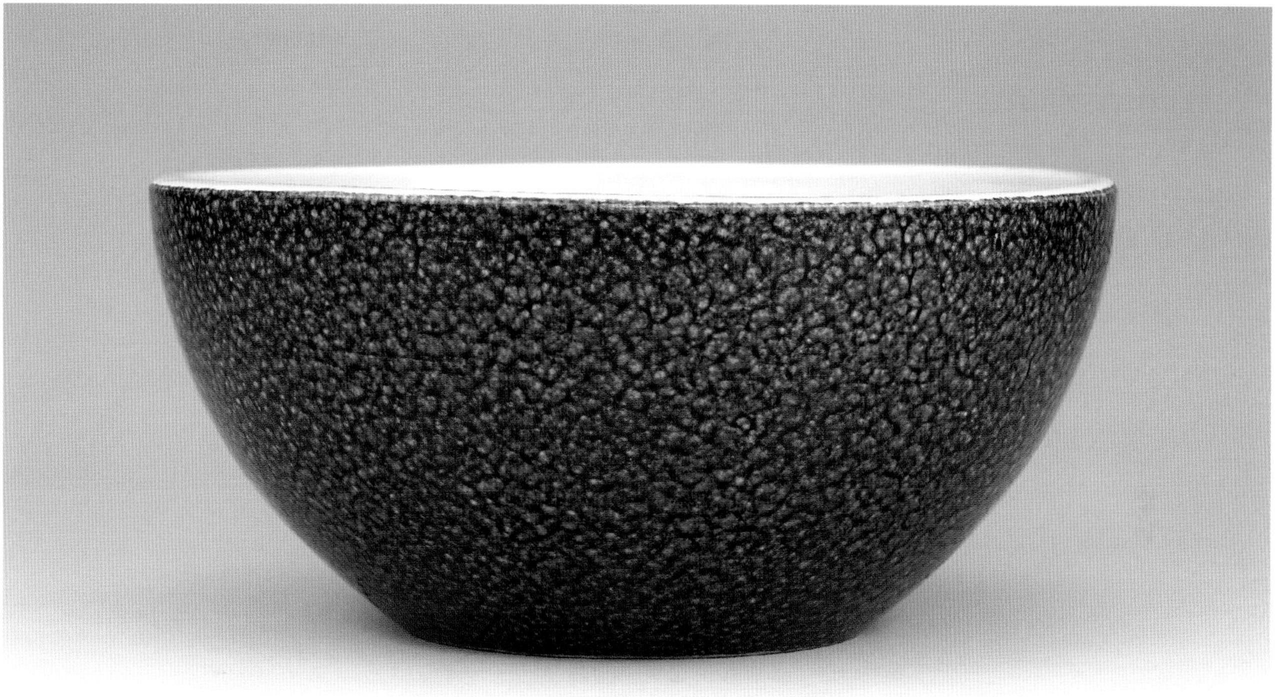

34 Bowl with 'snowflake blue' glaze
Jingdezhen, Jiangxi province 江西省，景德鎮
Ming dynasty, Xuande mark and period, AD 1426–35
Height 11.5 cm; diameter 25.2 cm
PDF 605

The shape of this thickly potted bowl and its glaze were an innovation of the Xuande emperor's reign. The exterior of the twice-fired bowl is covered with a blown-on 'snowflake blue' or speckled blue effect. 'Snowflake blue' [雪花藍 , *xuehualan*] is a low-temperature (about 800°C) lead-fluxed glaze, coloured with cobalt oxide. Traditionally Chinese connoisseurs, collectors and scholars employed this poetic term to describe the appearance of mottled white splodges that resemble snowflakes amid the tones of blue in the glaze. Extant examples of 'snowflake blue' glazed porcelain are very rare. Excavations have yielded sherds of *meiping* vases, bowls, narcissus bowls and stem cups decorated in this style, which may have been experimental. In the centre inside is inscribed a six-character blue reign mark of the Xuande emperor beneath a transparent glaze. Both the base and its shallow broad foot ring are unglazed. An identical bowl was excavated at the imperial kilns in Jingdezhen in 1983. Some scholars believe this type of *bo* bowl was used as a receptacle for throwing dice in a game.

35 Saucer-dish with flowering pomegranate

Jingdezhen, Jiangxi province 江西省，景德鎮
Ming dynasty, Xuande mark and period, AD 1426–35
Height 5.5 cm; diameter 29.5 cm
PDF A755

This porcelain dish is decorated in uneven underglaze-blue tones, with the cobalt oxide having fired black in some areas and pale blue in others. The design delineates a flowering pomegranate branch in the centre with fruiting branches of persimmon, peach, lychee and cherry in the walls. The branches have ragged ends, following a well-known convention indicating they were broken from a tree. The larger leaves are painted to suggest curling at the edges, contrasting with the younger growth. On the exterior are four stylized blue lotus flowers and a six-character Xuande reign mark written horizontally at the rim. The yellow glaze is faintly iridescent like oil on water and it appears worn, with tiny rubbed and scratched patches all over. The base is unglazed and speckled with tiny brown flecks. Official porcelain production at the imperial kilns in Jingdezhen was prolific during the Xuande emperor's short ten-year reign. Literally millions of porcelain tablewares and ritual vessels were made. The kilns' output was staggering in terms of quantity but also with regard to quality of glaze and variety of forms. This design, invented in the early fifteenth century, was made continuously for a hundred years at Jingdezhen and was later revived in the Qing dynasty (AD 1644–1911).

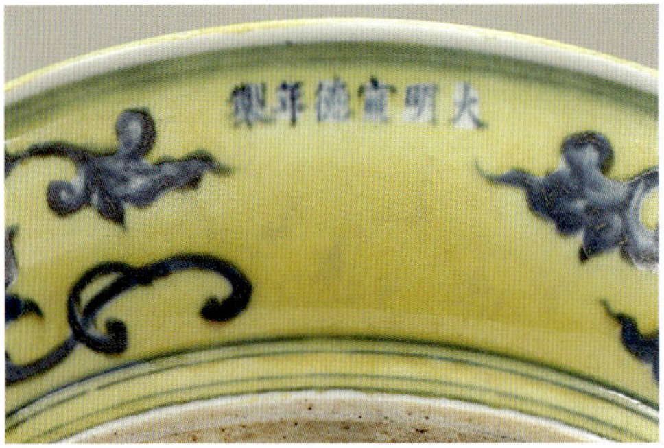

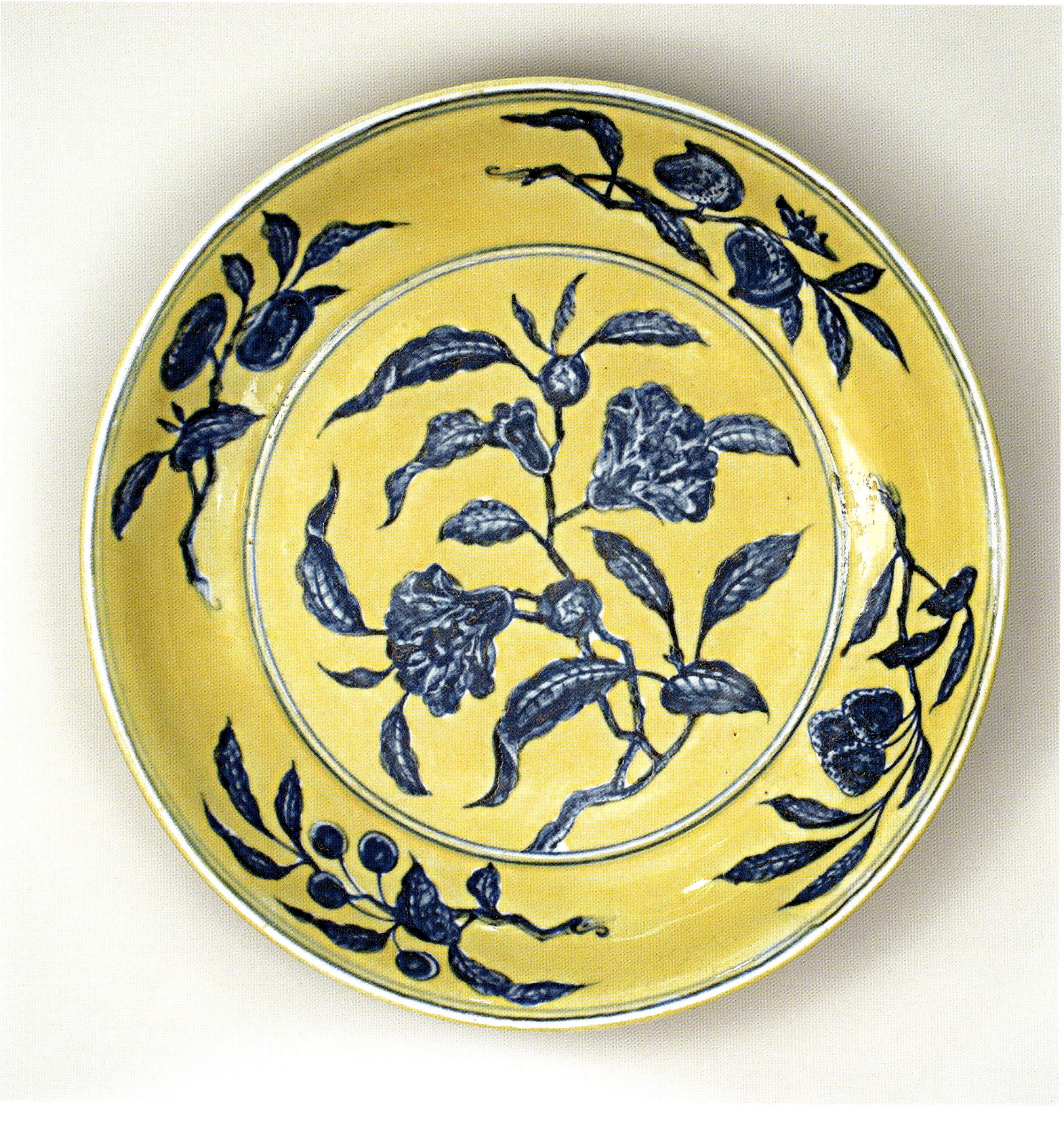

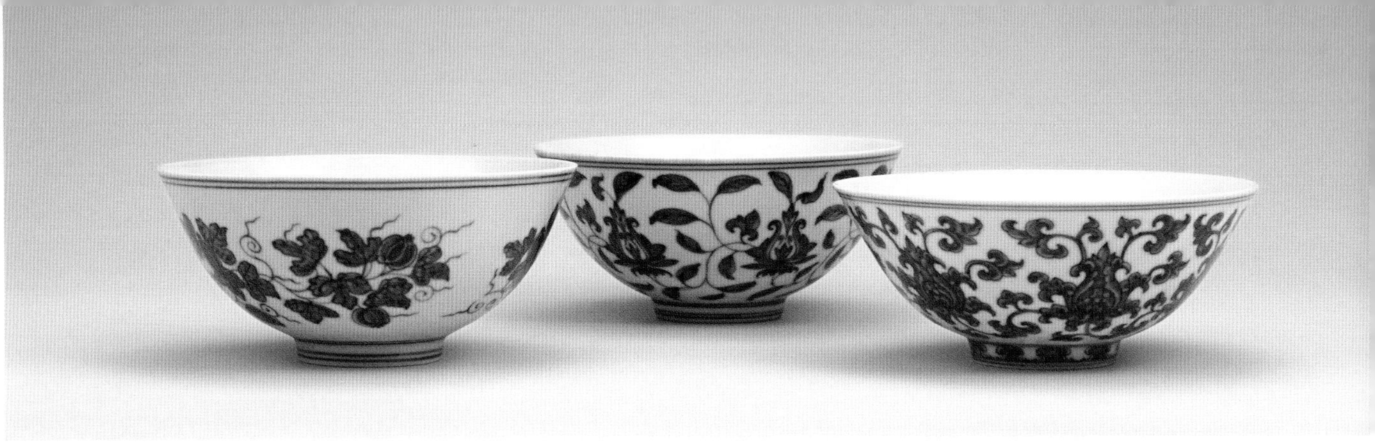

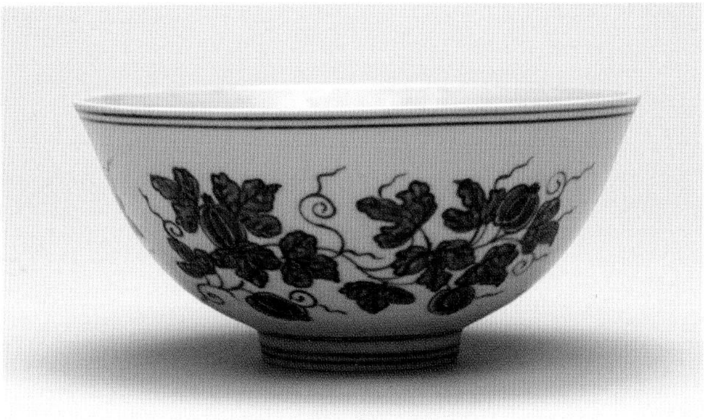

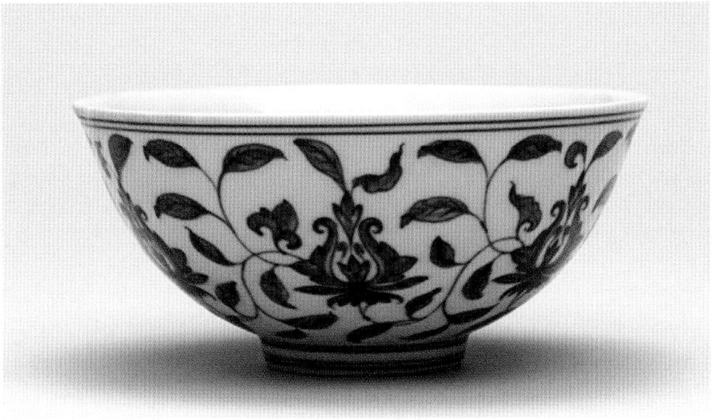

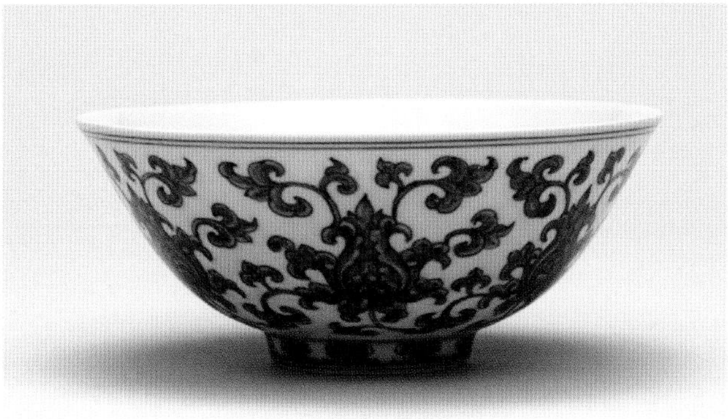

36 Seven blue-and-white 'palace bowls'
Jingdezhen, Jiangxi province 江西省，景德鎮
Ming dynasty, Chenghua mark and period, AD 1465–87
Heights max. 7.2 cm; diameters max. 15.5 cm
PDF A644, A646–A650 and B681

In the Chenghua era production of porcelain at the imperial kilns at Jingdezhen was on a much smaller scale than in the earlier Xuande period (AD 1426–35). Although the later era was almost twice as long as the former, fewer than half as many porcelains have been found in the Chenghua strata at the imperial kilns. Shapes and decorative schemes were less innovative than before but Chenghua porcelain achieved a new delicacy and purity so that large areas were left free of decoration in order that the whiteness of the porcelain could be admired. Blue-and-white Chenghua mark and period bowls of the type seen here were first called 'palace

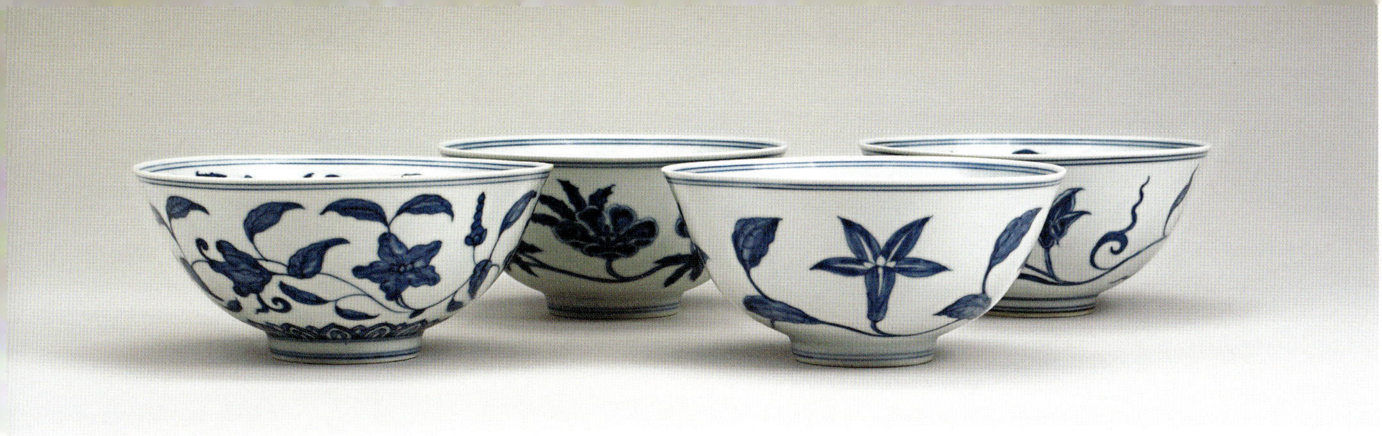

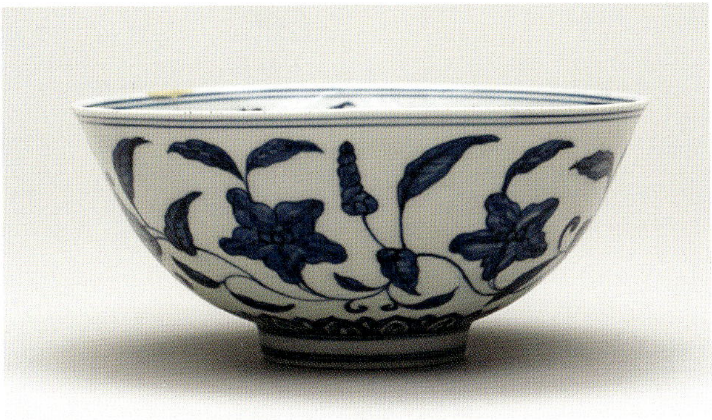

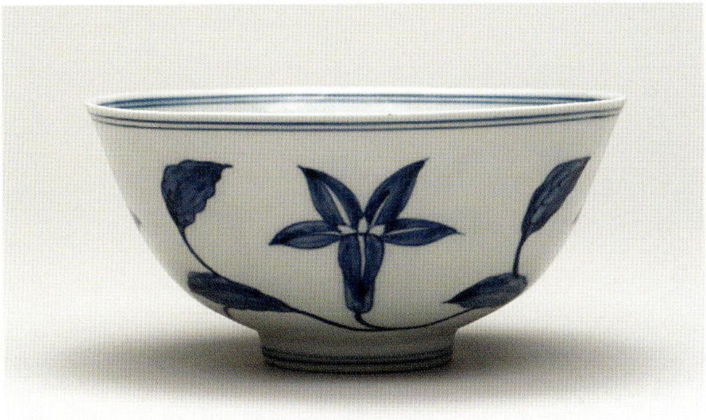

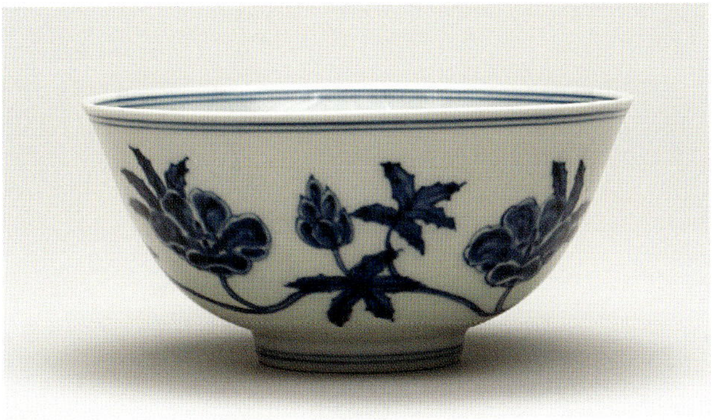

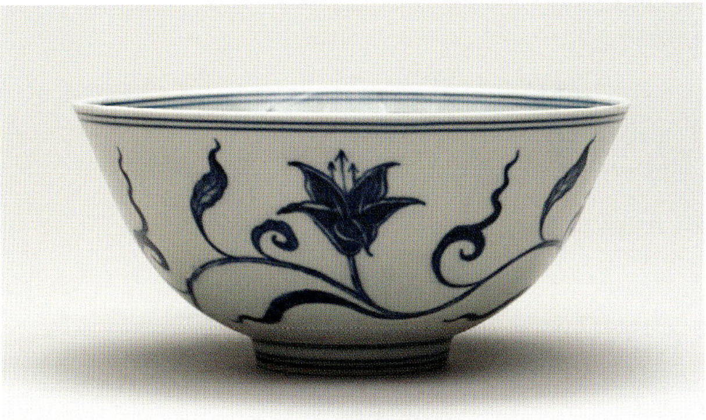

bowls' in print by the sinologist and former British Museum curator Archibald Brankston (AD 1909–41) in 1938 in his seminal work, *Early Ming Wares of Chingtechen* (Jingdezhen). The blue-and-white designs include lily scrolls, mallows, stylized lotus flowers, gardenia and fruiting melon vines.

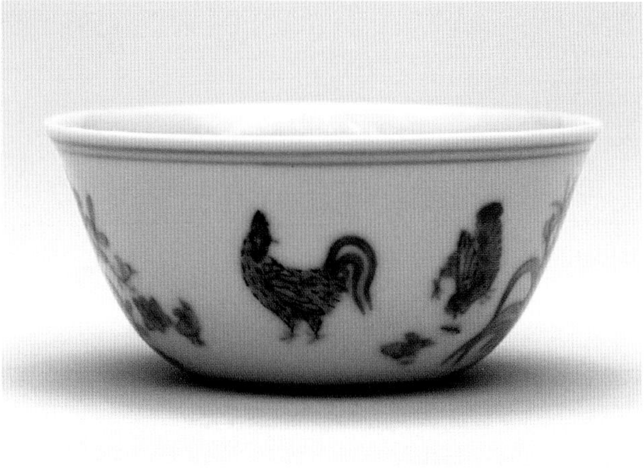

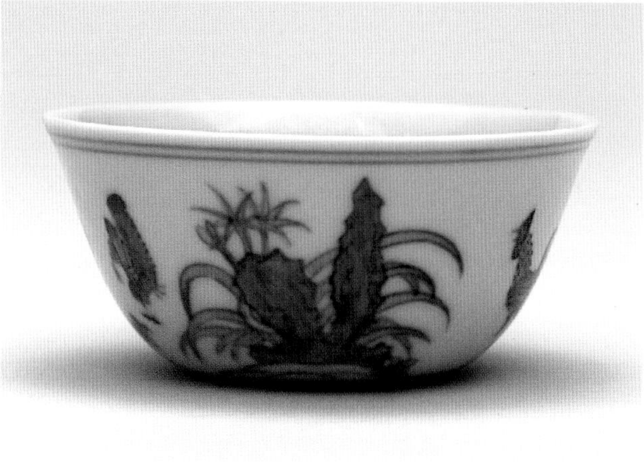

37 *Doucai* chicken cup

Jingdezhen, Jiangxi province 江西省，景德鎮

Ming dynasty, Chenghua mark and period, AD 1465–87

Height 3.8 cm; diameter 8.3 cm

PDF A748

In China, an image of a cockerel is regarded as auspicious. Artists first depicted in paintings the theme of a hen pecking for food with her chicks by rocks and flowers, and these inspired the porcelain versions. Ts'ai Ho-pi, the Taiwanese scholar, cites a painting of a hen foraging for food with her offspring by an anonymous Song dynasty artist in the National Palace Museum's collection. This bears an admiring commentary written by the Chenghua emperor in AD 1486. Decorators used layers of coloured enamels to suggest different textures: for example the cockerels' feathers are indicated with tiny red strokes and the hen's wing is outlined in red against her yellow feathers. This is several hundred years before the development of a palette of opaque enamels that would allow shading. The scene shows real movement. One chick is depicted flapping its fluffy yellow wings in an effort to rejoin the group. Copies of Chenghua chicken cups have been made continuously from the sixteenth century to the present day. Genuine Chenghua porcelain has a mild yellowish cast, is slightly irregular in form, and the composition of birds and chicks is well balanced.

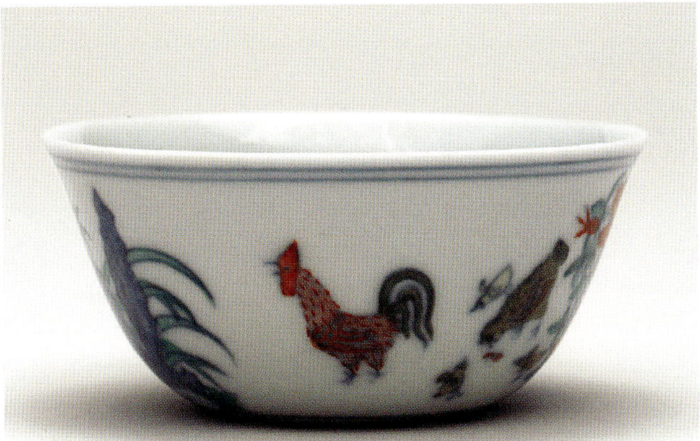
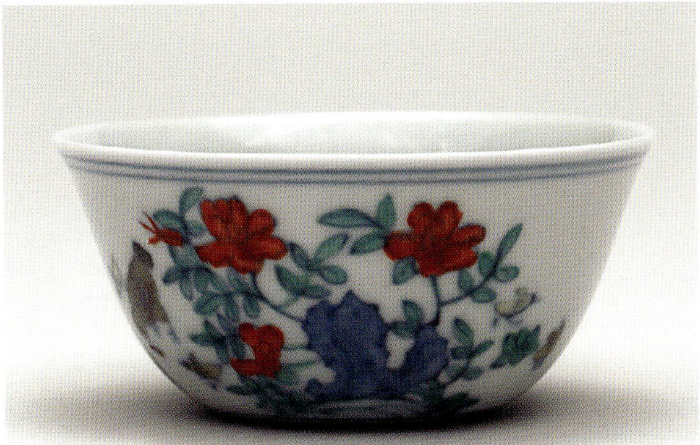
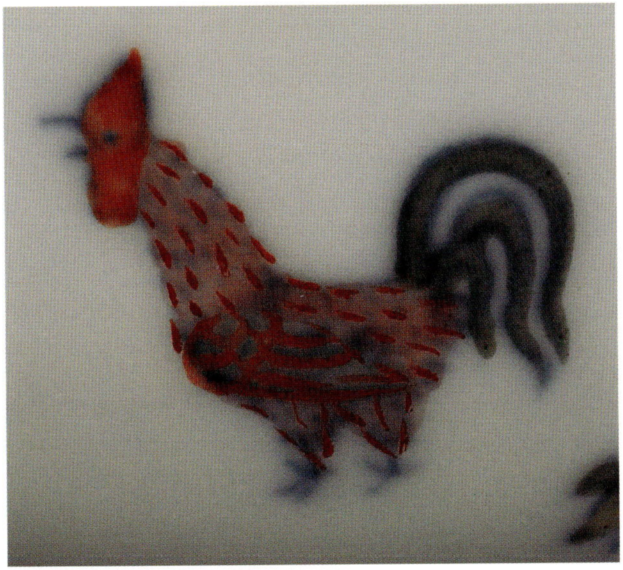
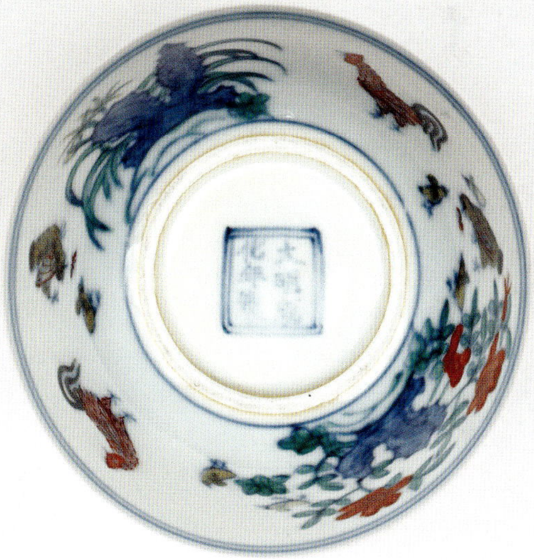

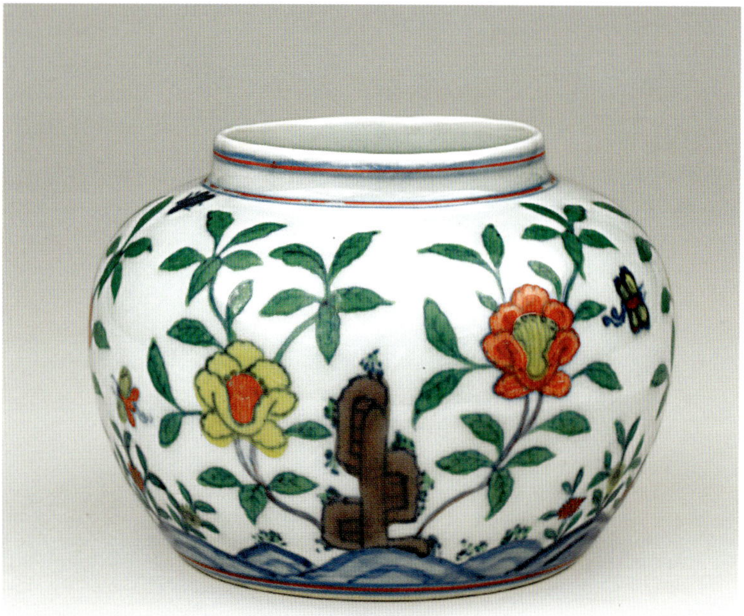

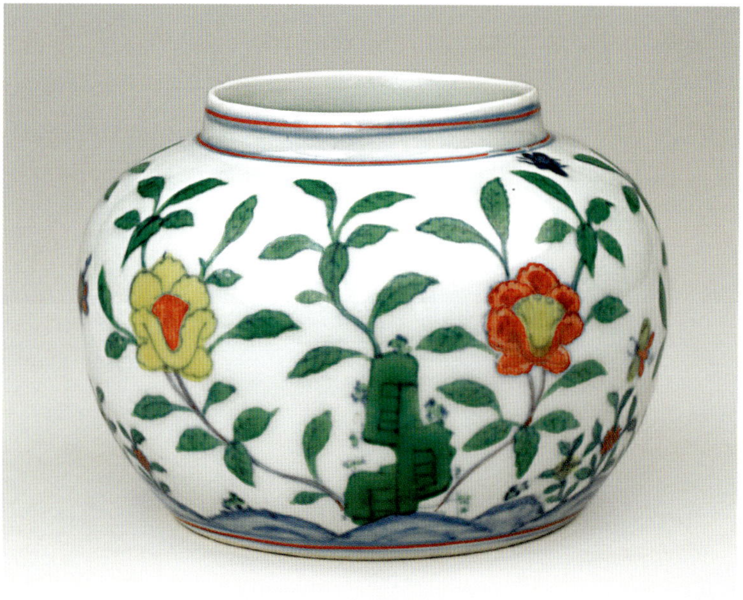

38 *Doucai* jar with camellias and rocks

Jingdezhen, Jiangxi province 江西省，景德鎮

Ming dynasty, Chenghua mark and period, AD 1465–87

Height 9.1 cm

PDF 797

Doucai [interlocking colours] is a decorative technique used here in which outlines are painted directly on to the leather-hard porcelain body in cobalt. Then the vessel is glazed and fired. Next the outlined designs are filled in with enamel colours and the piece is refired in a muffle kiln at a lower temperature. This particular twice-fired technique was first used in the early fifteenth century but was perfected in the Chenghua era. This type of ovoid jar is extremely rare and is decorated with a repeated design of three rocks in aubergine, green and yellow enamel respectively, each flanked by camellias with butterflies in between. On the base is a six-character underglaze-blue Chenghua reign mark.

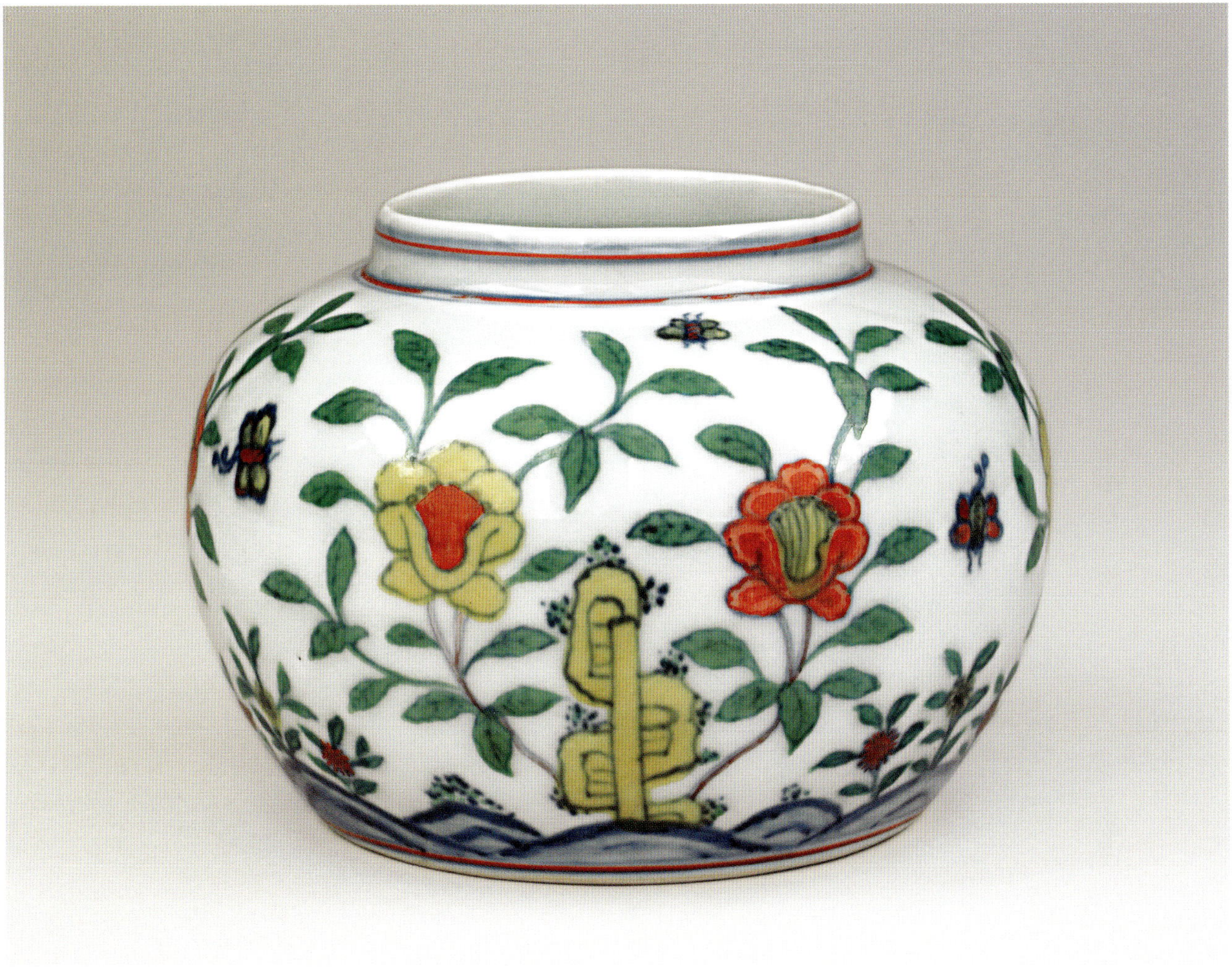

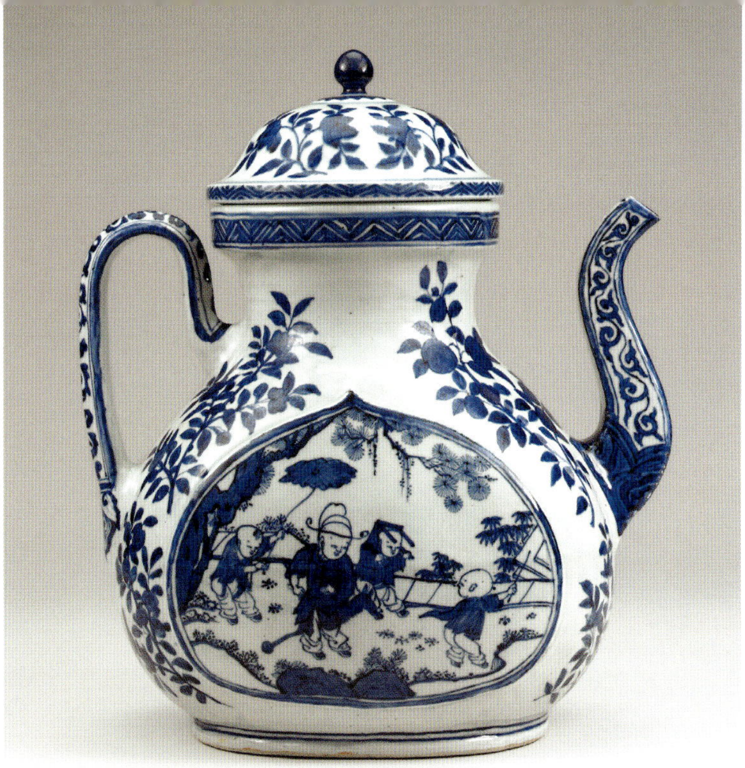

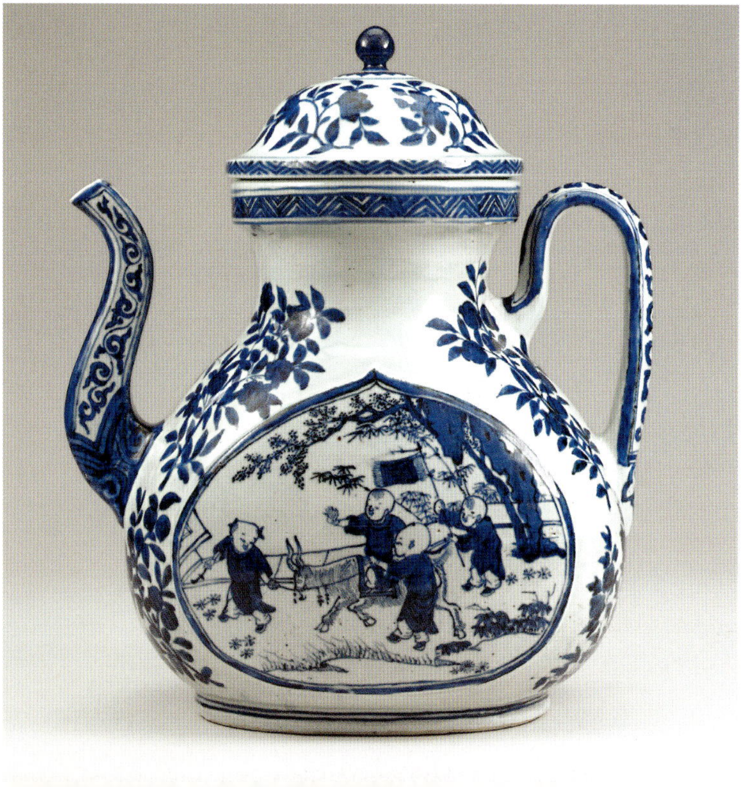

39 Blue-and-white covered ewer with children playing

Jingdezhen, Jiangxi province 江西省，景德鎮
Ewer: Ming dynasty, Jiajing mark and period, AD 1522–66, cover Qing dynasty, AD 1736-95
Height 29.2 cm; width 24.6 cm
PDF B617

Blue used for imperial wares during the second half of the sixteenth century has a very strong, dark and even tone. Here it is skilfully used to depict scenes of boys processing in gardens, framed within peach-shaped panels, on either side of the porcelain ewer. A smiling boy, wearing an official's hat, is depicted riding a hobby horse. He is playing at being a successful scholar-official mounted on a horse and is accompanied by three smaller boys who play the part of his servants. One carries a lotus leaf as a parasol to shade him from the sun; another carries a stool in case he tires of riding; and the third proclaims the grand boy's arrival with a stick. On the other side, a boy is shown riding a goat that is being led by its bridle, while another boy walks alongside and a fourth brandishes a flying banner. The Chinese regard genre scenes of children playing as auspicious, representing a wish for many sons. The base carries a six-character Jiajing reign mark within a double circle.

40 Jar and cover with dragons and a phoenix

Jingdezhen, Jiangxi province 江西省，景德鎮

Ming dynasty, Wanli mark and period, AD 1573–1620

Height 17.3 cm

PDF 795

Potters incised the unglazed but dried porcelain body with a five-clawed dragon on one side and on the cover, and a phoenix with a five-feathered tail on the other side, both among flowering plants. In a technique new to Jingdezhen, porcelain decorators applied the enamel directly to the biscuit-fired clay body rather than applying the enamels over the glaze. First yellow, then green enamel colours were added to the design. We know the order of the enamel application because the green overlaps the yellow at the edges of the motifs. In the Ming and Qing dynasties (AD 1368–1911) phoenix and dragon designs symbolized the emperor and empress. On the base is a six-character Wanli reign mark in underglaze blue. Although potters first experimented with this colour combination nearly two hundred years earlier in the Yongle period, the application of green and yellow enamel, without a base coating of glaze, is innovative.

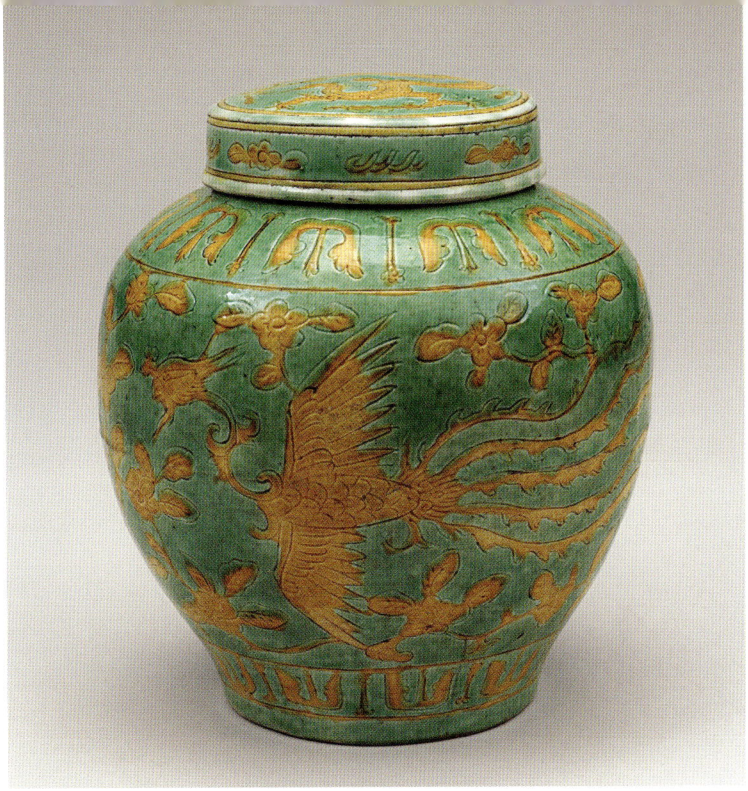

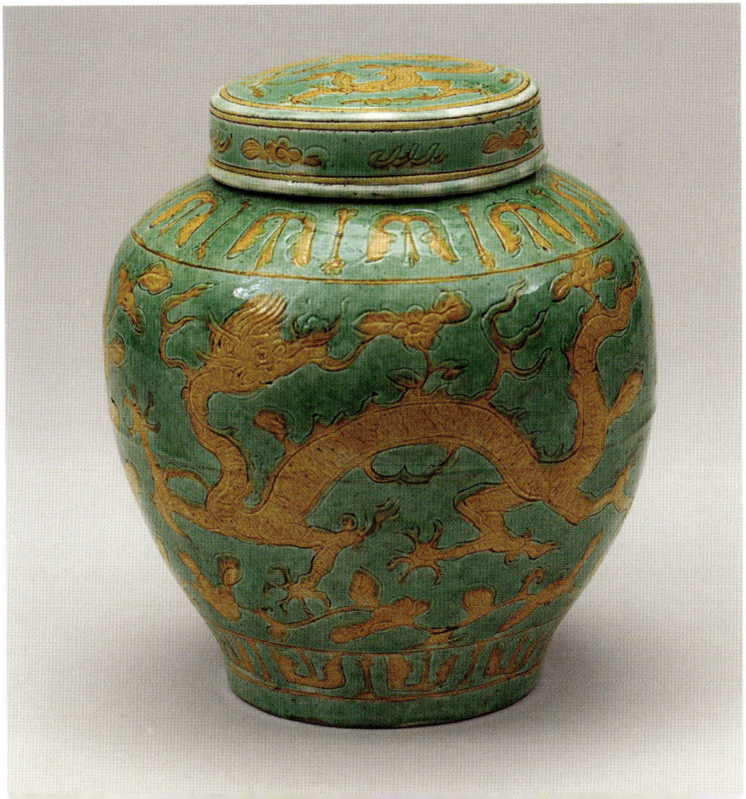

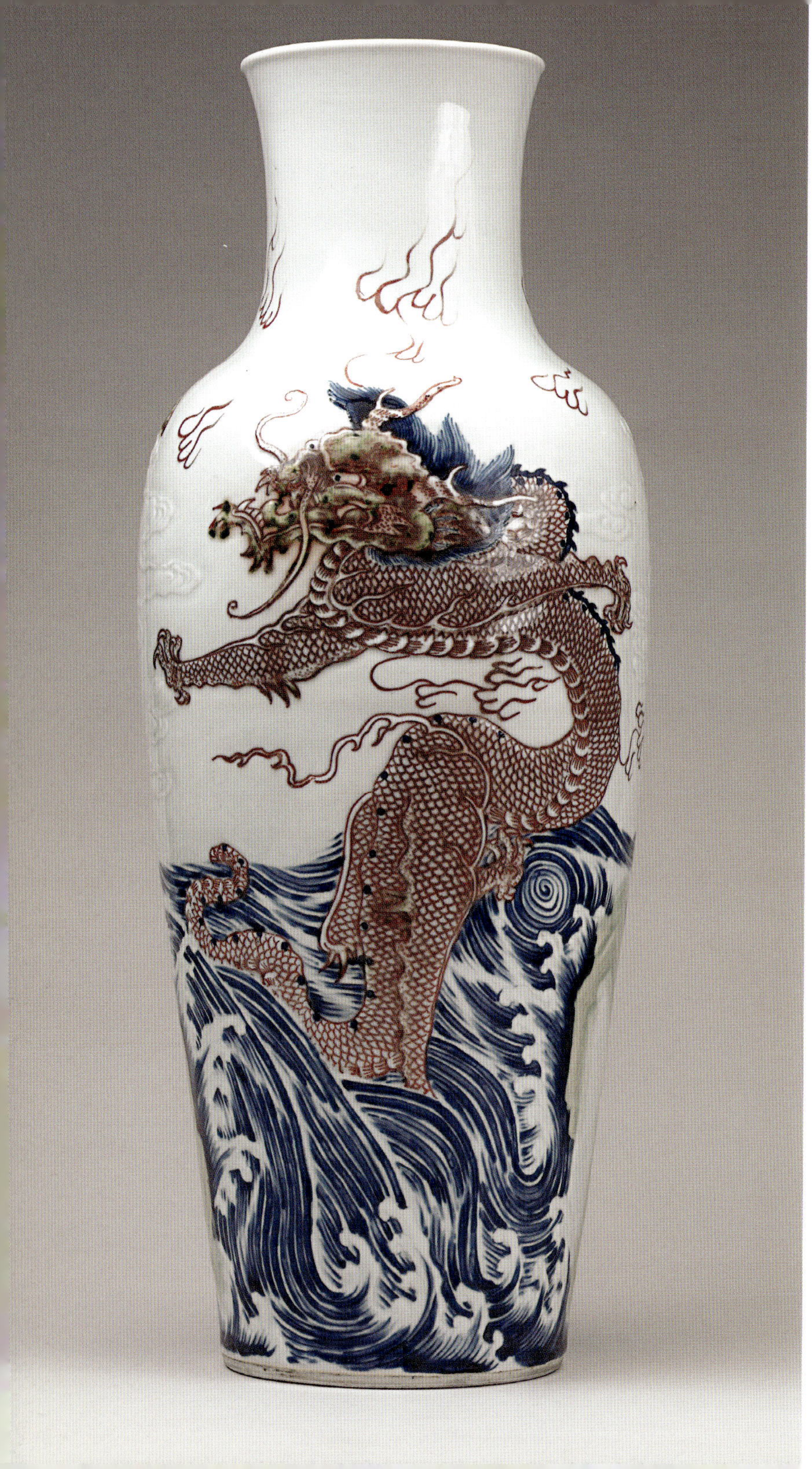

41 Vase showing dragons among waves
Jingdezhen, Jiangxi province 江西省，景德鎮
Qing dynasty, Kangxi mark and period,
AD 1662–1722
Height 42.1 cm
PDF C644

Porcelain painters demonstrated their virtuosity by combining three difficult to control high-fired colours in order to decorate this vase, a level of technical achievement that reflects close court patronage and supervision. The design was carved into the porcelain body in shallow relief and then copper red was added to the two four-clawed dragons, underglaze cobalt blue for the crashing waves, dragons' manes and spines, and iron-pigmented celadon for the outer edges of the rocks. To make the dragons appear more realistic they coloured the eyes with cobalt blue and to look more fanciful gave them blue dots down their backs. Although the technique of combining underglaze-red and -blue painting was first used more than three hundred years earlier by the Yuan dynasty potters at the same kiln site, Jingdezhen (see no. 23), the addition of celadon glaze to these was an innovation of the late seventeenth century. The Kangxi emperor ordered this vase and its base bears his six-character underglaze-blue reign mark, arranged in three rows of two characters within a double ring.

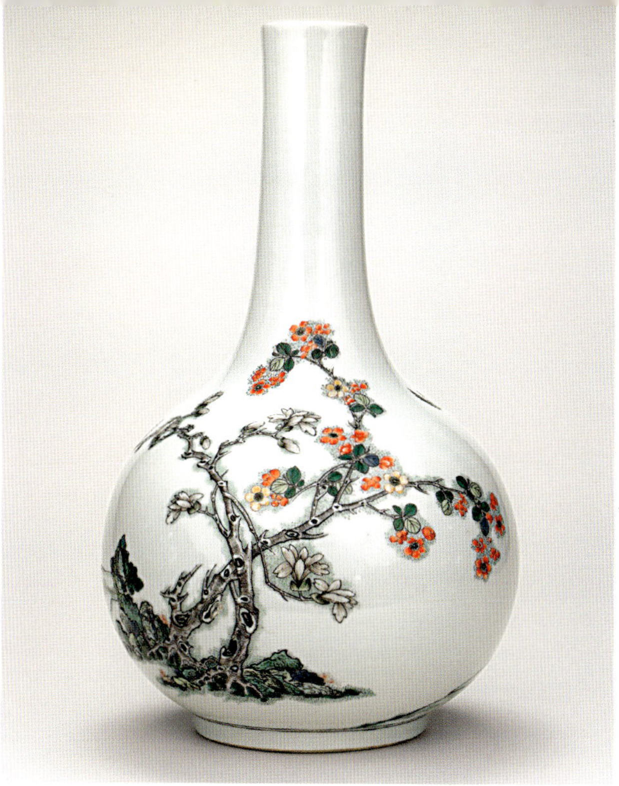 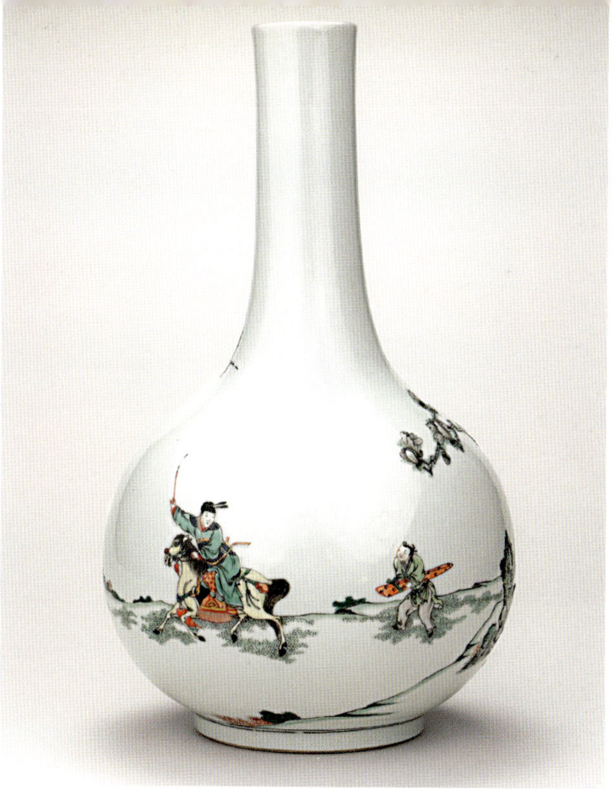

42 Vase with horseman
Jingdezhen, Jiangxi province 江西省，景德鎮
Qing dynasty, Yongzheng mark and period, AD 1723–35
Height 36.5 cm
PDF 823

This vase is decorated with a scholar-official on horseback, accompanied by his servant carrying a *qin* [zither] wrapped in a flower-patterned cloth. The rider holds his crop in the air, pointing to a pair of flying birds that emerge from intertwined prunus and magnolia trees. Dr Ni Yibin, a contemporary Chinese scholar, suggests the scene may be an illustration of lines by the Tang poet Meng Jiao (AD 751–814) from his poem 'On Passing the Imperial Examinations':

> On my cantering horse in the spring breeze, my eyes joyfully devoured all the blossoms in the capital Chang'an in a single day.

Potters carved the design in low relief to make it more dramatic and added enamel colours over the glaze, using green wash shading to add volume and tiny black dots to suggest texture. This translucent watercolour-like palette, characterized by shades of green, black, red and yellow, and the relief carving style are rare in the period of the Yongzheng emperor but were highly popular in the reign of his father Kangxi (AD 1662–1722). From around 1720, porcelain decorators used opaque enamels with a true pink, as opposed to the pale coral red.

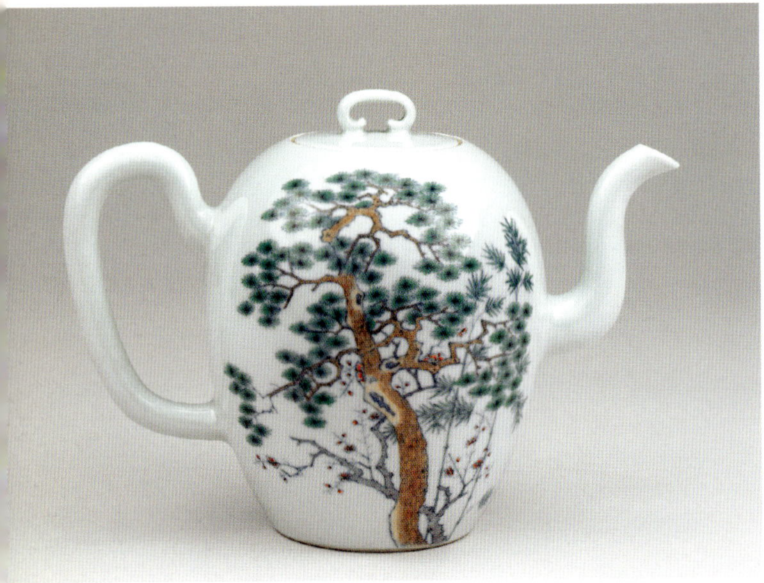

43 Ewer with *doucai* decoration
Jingdezhen, Jiangxi province 江西省，景德鎮
Qing dynasty, Yongzheng mark and period, AD 1723–35
Height 13.7 cm
PDF A798

This porcelain ewer is decorated in Qing dynasty (AD 1644–1911) *doucai* [interlocking colours] style with underglaze blue outlines and washes and overglaze green, aubergine and brown enamel. The prunus blossoms are highlighted with tiny dots of red enamel. Chinese people read this design of pine, bamboo and prunus as the 歲寒三友, *suihan sanyou* [The Three Friends of Winter]. Pine trees are evergreen and grow for a long time, representing stability and longevity; bamboo, another evergreen, symbolizes the educated Confucian, an ideal gentleman-scholar who should be like a bamboo stem, bending rather than breaking in adverse conditions; and the plum stands for purity as well as leadership, because it is the first flower to bloom in China in the New Year. There is a six-character Yongzheng seal mark in underglaze blue on the base.

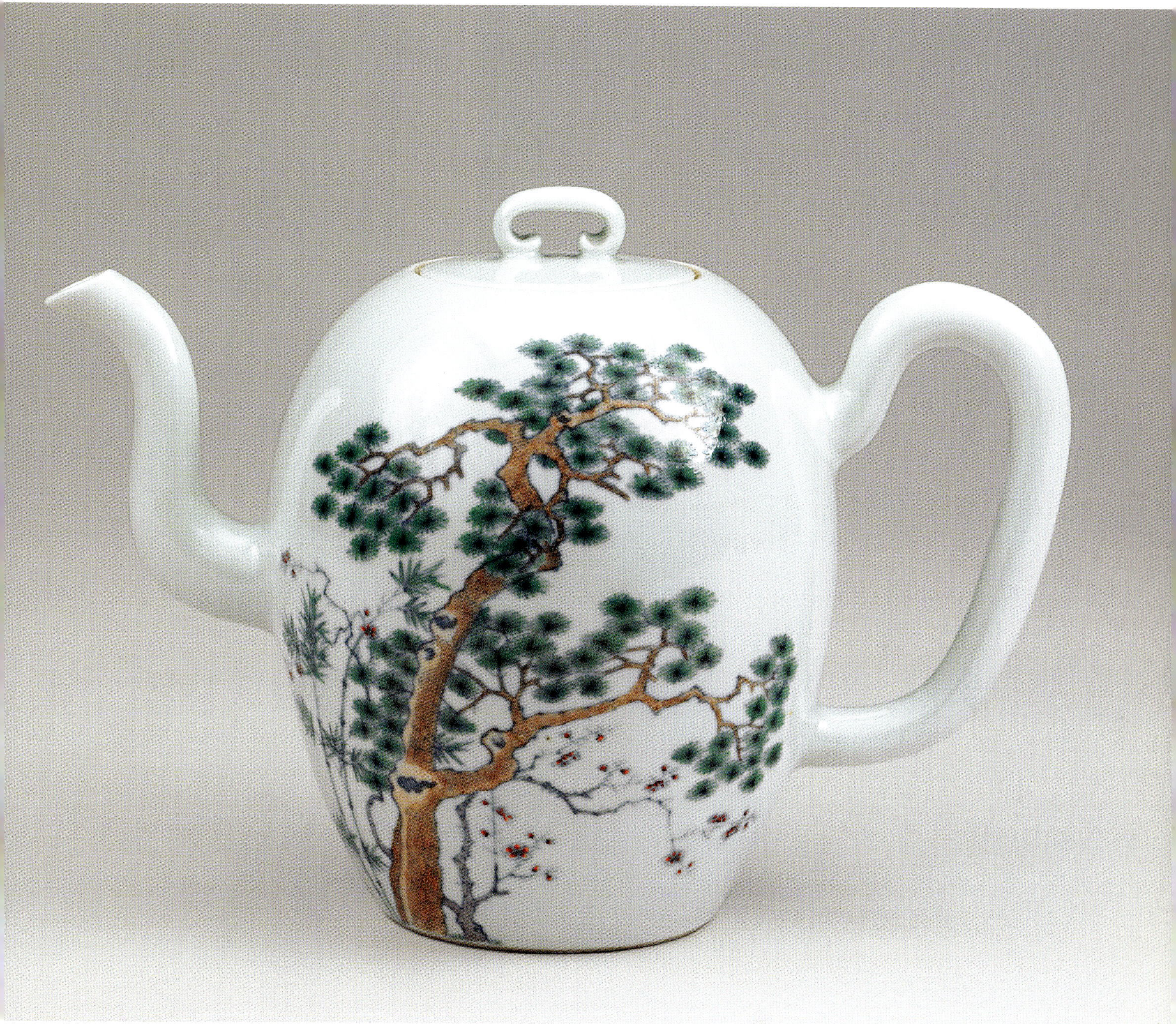

44 Moon flask with pairs of birds on flowering branches

Jingdezhen, Jiangxi province 江西省，景德鎮

Qing dynasty, Yongzheng mark and period, AD 1723–35

Height 29.3 cm

PDF 824

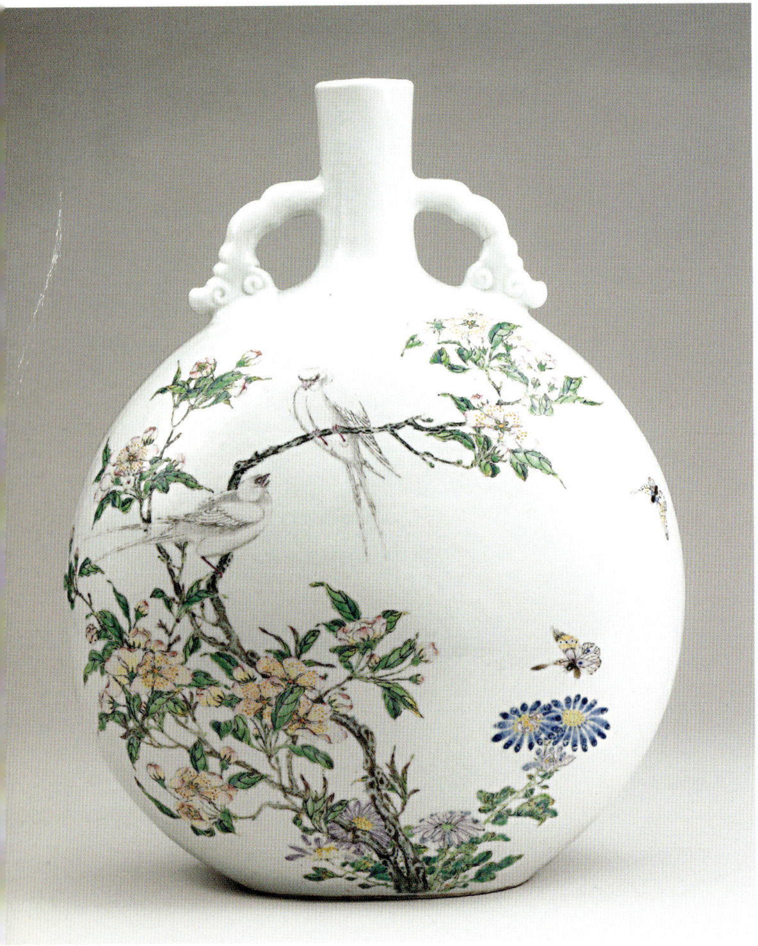

Although the shape of this moon flask with its flattened round body, tubular neck and cloud scroll handles is archaic, as is its basic design, referring to the porcelain *bian hu* flasks first made at Jingdezhen for the Yongle emperor (AD 1403–24) (see no. 28 right), the *famille rose* decoration in terms of both its palette and technical skill is innovative to the Yongzheng reign. On one side, two *bai tou weng* [literally white-headed old man] birds are shown on the branches of a white and pink flowering branch, and on the other side a pair of white birds is shown perched in a different type of blossoming tree with a pair of butterflies fluttering above blue and purple asters. The detail used in the painting is remarkable, reflecting both the court commissioning of this piece and the supervision of its manufacture at the imperial kilns at Jingdezhen. Each group of naturalistic leaves is composed of up to four different shades of green and the shading on the blossoms is extraordinarily well defined. New colours include a blue enamel, which replaces underglaze blue for the asters, a white enamel for the birds' wings, and puce for the birds' legs and beaks. The *bai tou weng* birds are a rebus for *bai tou fu gui* [white haired (in old age) (may you enjoy) riches and honour]. The base carries an underglaze-blue six-character Yongzheng seal mark.

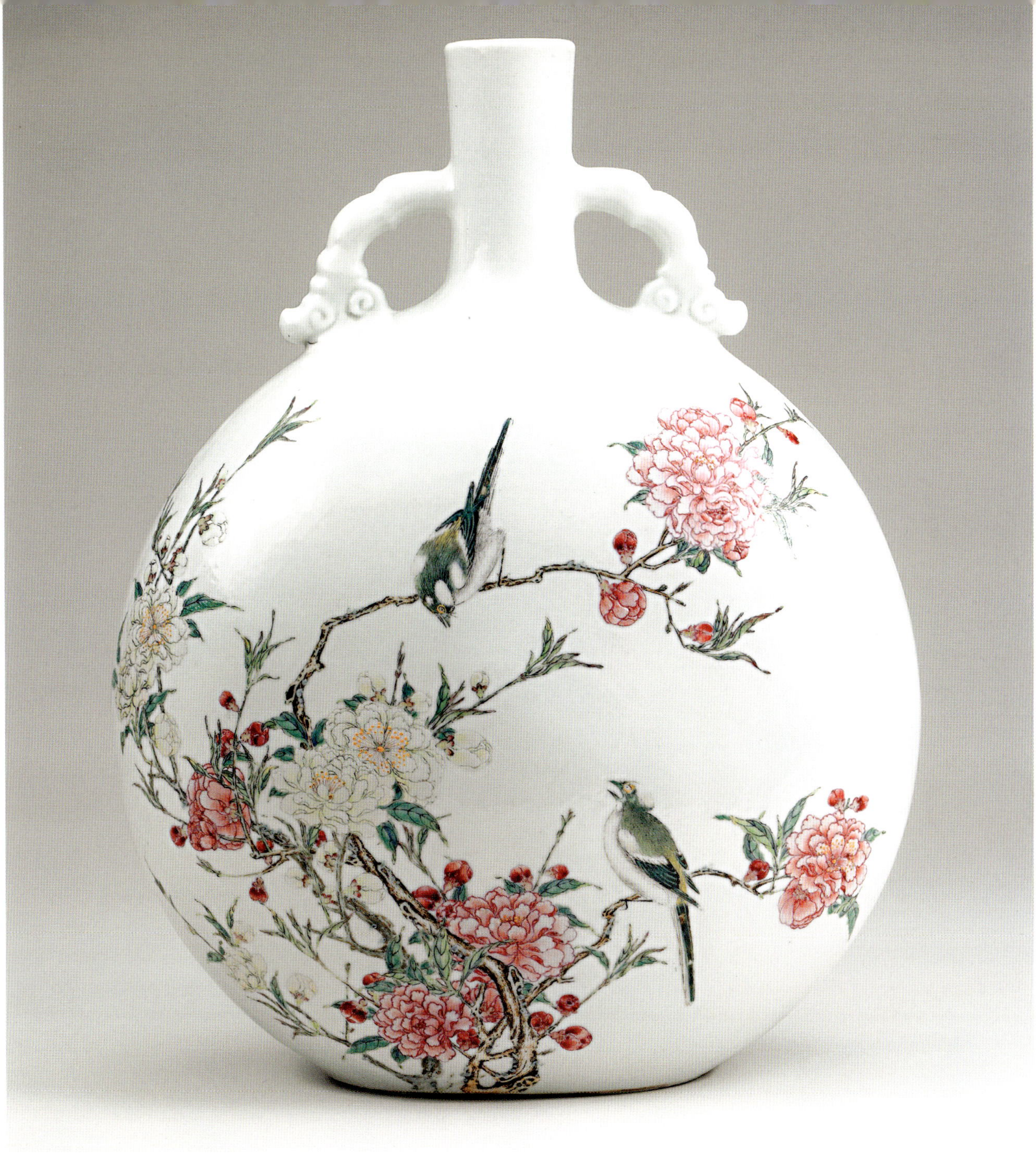

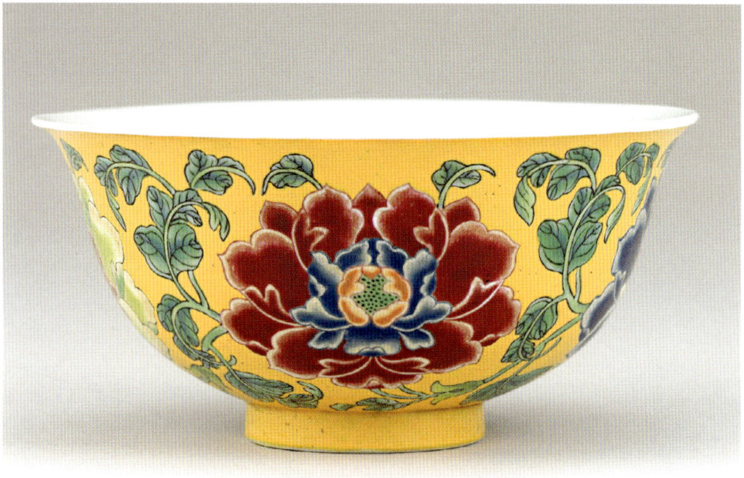

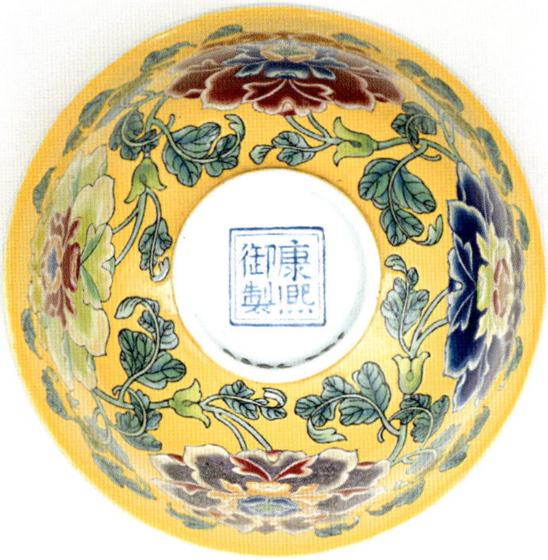

45 Bowl with peonies
Porcelain made in Jingdezhen, Jiangxi province; decoration added in Beijing
素瓷器：江西景德鎮燒製；北京加琺瑯彩
Qing dynasty, Kangxi *yuzhi* mark and period, about AD 1716–22
Height 5.6 cm; diameter 11.5 cm
PDF A806

The Kangxi emperor set up enamel workshops within the Forbidden City for decorating porcelain, copper and glass. He was inspired to do so by a desire to reproduce European styles of enamel work that he had seen through his contact with foreign Jesuits resident in China trying to convert the population to Catholicism. The imperial household department ran these workshops and ordered superior-quality, clear-glazed white porcelains from the imperial kilns in Jingdezhen to be decorated in the palace in Beijing. The palette, textures and application of the enamels are rather different from those used at Jingdezhen (compare with no. 44). The Kangxi palace designs are formal and stylized as the court enamellers were influenced by enamelling on metal, which was already practised at the palace. Instead of the underglaze-blue reign mark used on porcelains completed at Jingdezhen, this bowl, typical of palace workshop decoration, is marked using overglaze blue enamel. Also, the character 年 [*nian*], meaning year, is here replaced by 御 [*yu*], meaning imperial. Thus the four-character mark 康熙御製 [*Kangxi yuzhi*] in a double square means made by imperial command of the Kangxi emperor.

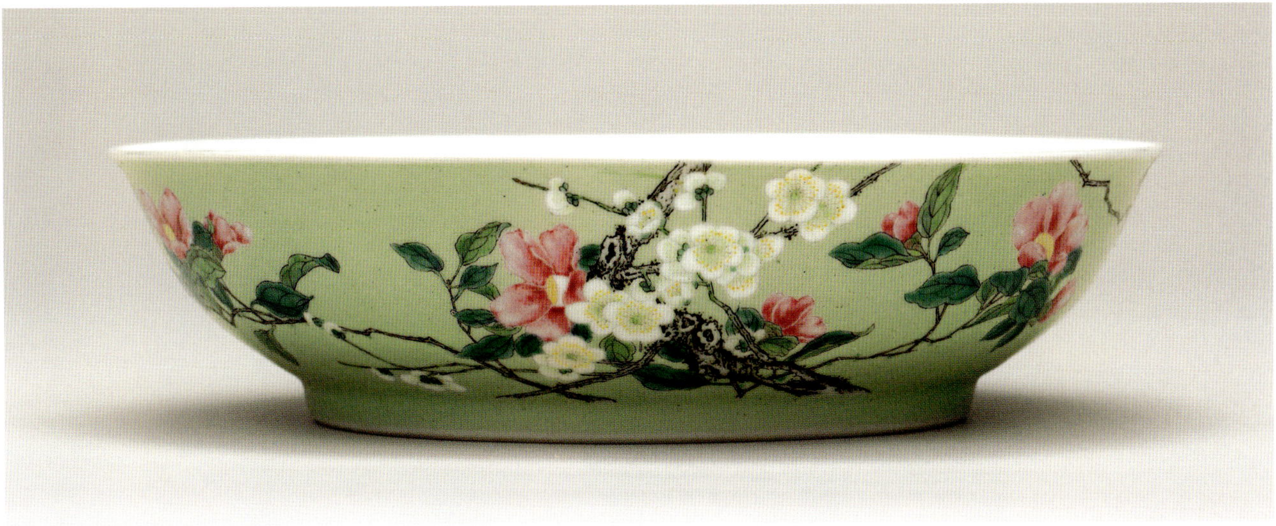

46 Saucer-dish with flowers and a poem
Porcelain made in Jingdezhen, Jiangxi province; decoration added in Beijing
素瓷器：江西景德鎮燒製；北京加琺瑯彩
Qing dynasty, Yongzheng mark and period, AD 1723–35
Height 4.4 cm; diameter 17.1 cm
PDF A808

Potters at the Jingdezhen imperial kilns made this fine white porcelain dish and sent it to the Forbidden City to be decorated in the imperial workshops. On one side is a design of intertwined branches of prunus and camellia in *falangcai* [foreign enamels], on the other side a complementary poem in black enamel that reads 淡妝疎影兩依依, *danzhuang shuying liang yiyi* [lightly adorned (casting) scattered shadows (they) both clink together]. This poem is from 《佩文齊詠物詩》(Peiwenzhai collection of poems) compiled by the Kangxi emperor in AD1706 in *juan* 86. The Yongzheng emperor pioneered the practice of using these poems for his porcelains. The three seals are the same as on no. 47. The bright lime-green ground colour was an innovation of the Yongzheng reign and was influenced by Western technology. The scientist Professor Edward T. Hall (1924–2001) analysed this lime-green glaze, revealing that it was made by adding copper to lead antimonate. Chinese potters made little use of lead antimonate, despite having large deposits of it, but in Europe it was used for a bright yellow pigment in glass, glaze and oil paint. On the base is a four-character Yongzheng *nianzhi* mark in a double square in blue enamel.

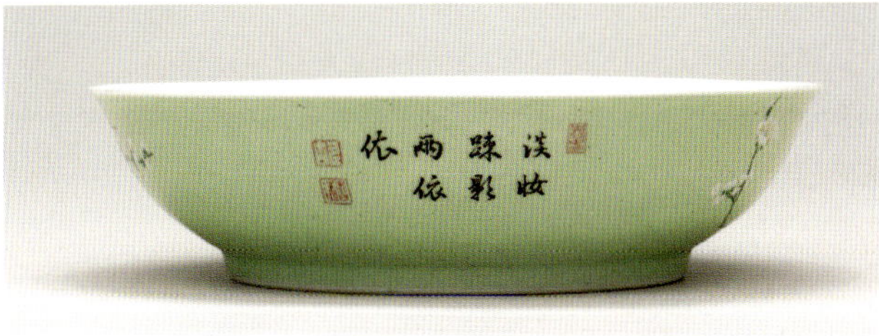

47 Bowls with prunus flowers and poems
Porcelain made in Jingdezhen, Jiangxi province; decoration added in Beijing
素瓷器：江西景德鎮燒製；北京加琺瑯彩
Qing dynasty, Yongzheng mark and period, AD 1723–35
Height 6.3 cm; diameter 12.7 cm
PDF 827 and PDF 828

Under court instructions, this pair of bowls was decorated in shades of black enamel with winter-flowering plum trees, a ten-character poem and three puce enamel seals. Sir Percival David bought them from Alfred E. Hippisley (1842–1940), a British customs official in China who translated the poem in 1900. A century later, the poem translates more literally as:

> 月幌見踈影，墨池聞暗香，*yue huang jian zhang ying; mo chi wen an xiang*
> The moon ripples (and I) see the shadow of a branch moving; at the ink-black pool you can smell the secret fragrance.

The seal before the poem reads 先春, *xian chun* [early spring], and the two after the poem read 古月, *guyue* [ancient moon] and 清香, *qingxiang* [pure fragrance]. The idea for the eighteenth-century poem may be based on lines by the poet Lin Pu (AD 965–1026), celebrated for throwing away his poems as soon as he had written them down as he cared nothing for fame. The flowering prunus painted in shades of black relates directly to traditional and contemporary Qing ink paintings.

These fine porcelain bowls are of an exceptional quality and rarity, seldom seen outside the imperial collections of the Palace Museums in Beijing and Taipei. Potters at the imperial kilns in Jingdezhen made the porcelain but painters decorated them in the Imperial Palace, Beijing, and fired them for a second time at a low temperature. Formerly scholars and collectors called these and other top-quality porcelains painted in the palace 古月軒器, *Gu Yue Xuan qi* [Pavilion of the Ancient Moon wares]. Although a seal *guyue* does appear on many of these pieces, recent research shows there was no such named pavilion in the Qing palace and the term is no longer widely used. Now they are known as 琺瑯彩 [*falangcai*, foreign colours] wares. On the base is a four-character Yongzheng *nianzhi* mark in a double square in blue enamel.

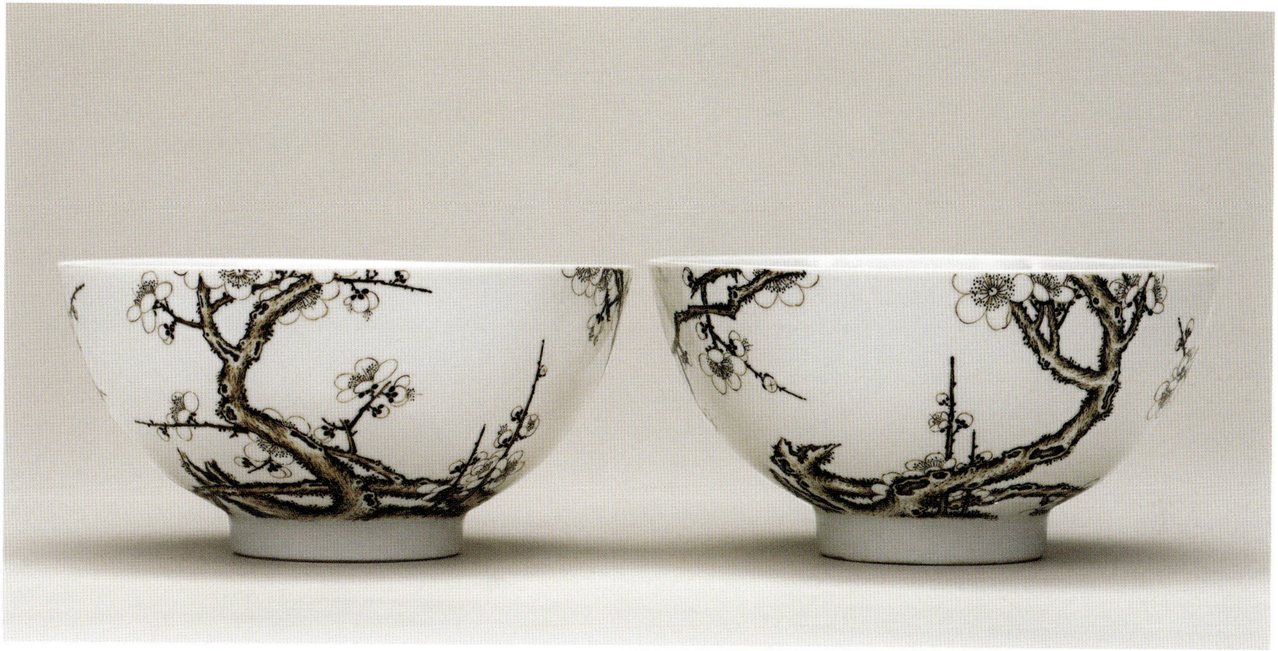

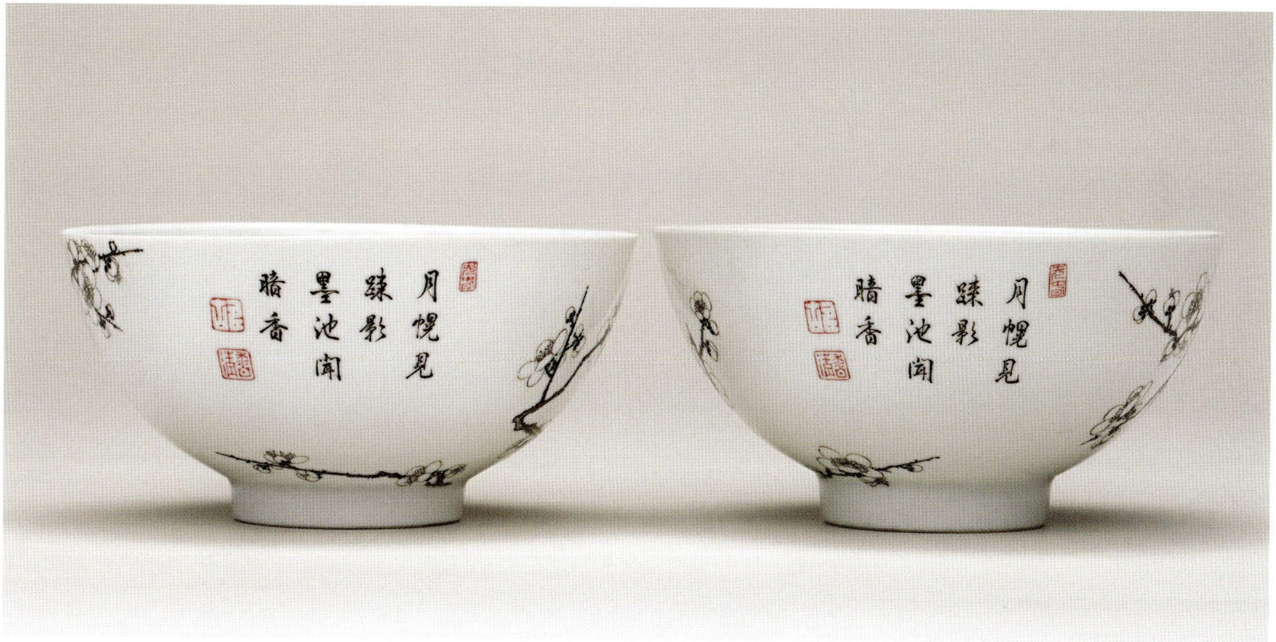
月幌見
踈影
墨池聞
暗香
月幌見
踈影
墨池聞
暗香

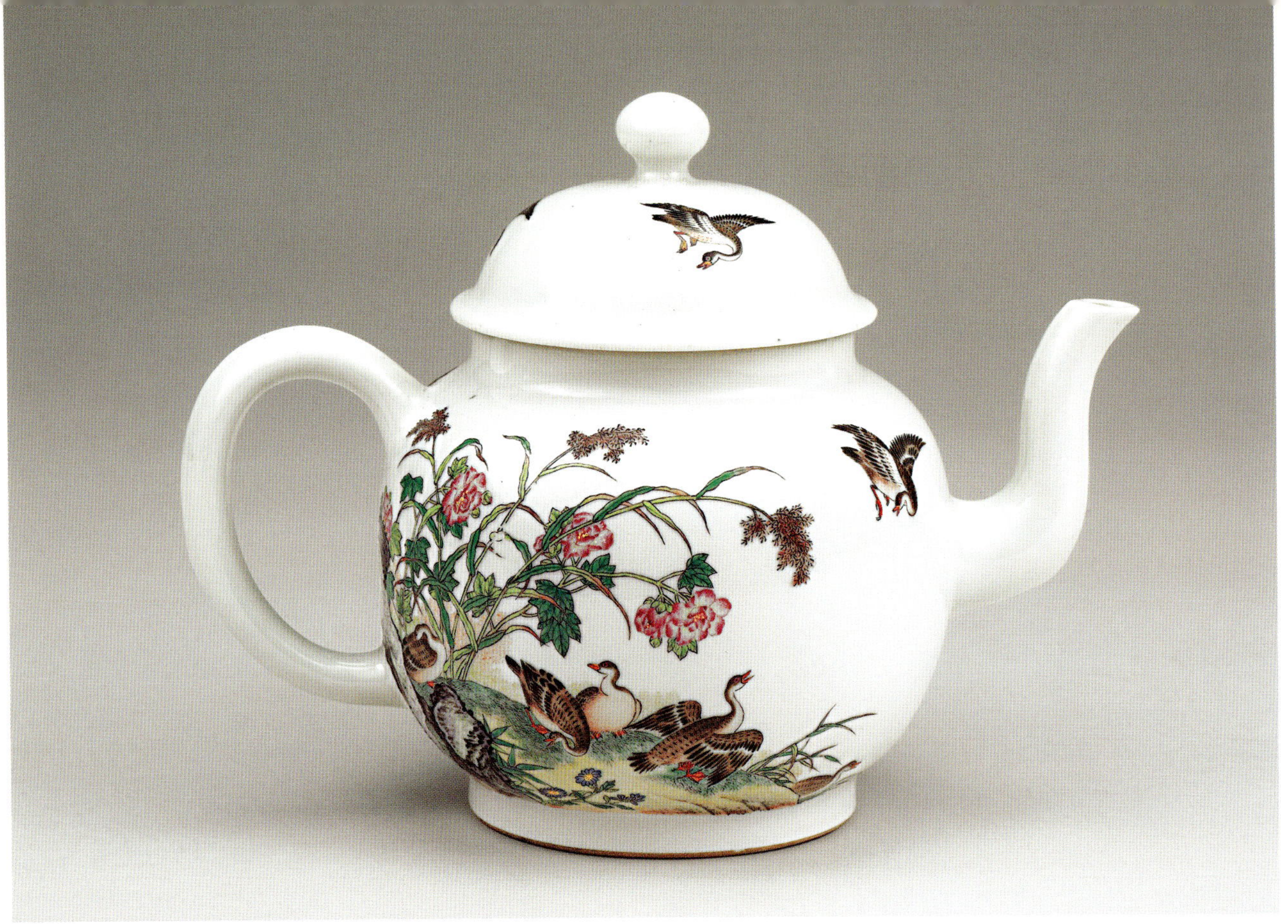

48 Teapot painted with geese and poem
Porcelain made in Jingdezhen, Jiangxi province; decoration added in Beijing
素瓷器：江西景德鎮燒製；北京加琺瑯彩
Qing dynasty, Qianlong mark and period, AD 1736–95
Height 13.4 cm
PDF A833

Porcelain painters in the Forbidden City painted geese, some taking flight, on a riverbank or lake shore dotted with rocks, hibiscus, reeds and rushes. They used *falangcai* [foreign enamels] and also wrote a couplet in black enamel accompanied by three puce enamel seals. The poem reads:

> 秋滿江湖同飲啄，風喧蘆葦自飛鳴, *qiu man jiang hu tong yin zhuo; feng xuan lu wei zi fei ming*
> Full autumn, together (the birds) drink and peck by rivers and lakes; in the wind the clamour of rushes and reeds flying around (sounds like) a bird's cry.

The first phrase is literal and describes the group of birds while the second phrase is more oblique and reflective. The three seals read 仁和, *renhe* [humanity and peace], 四方, *sifang* [four directions] and 清晏, *qingyan* [pure and

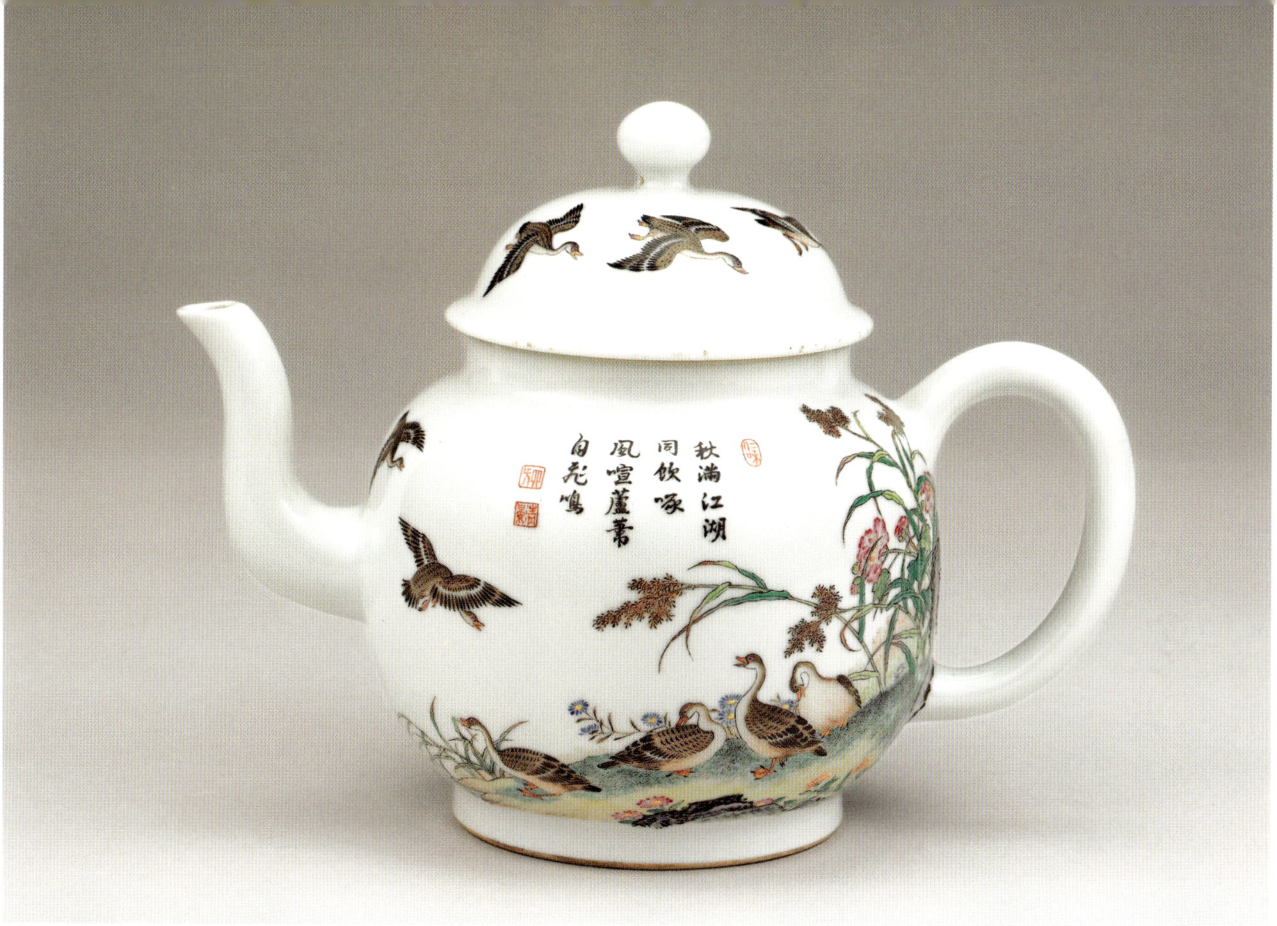

bright]. Together these make a statement of imperial power: humanity, peace and quietness throughout the four directions of the realm. Like a Chinese painting, the calligraphy and painting on this teapot complement each other. Usually teapots are not decorated on the underside of the lid but when this cover is turned over, two geese appear, one swimming, the other half-submerged as if diving for food beneath the water. The base carries a four-character blue enamel Qianlong reign mark.

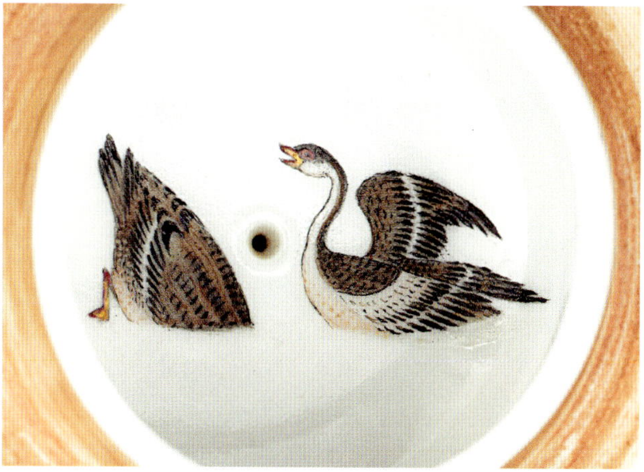

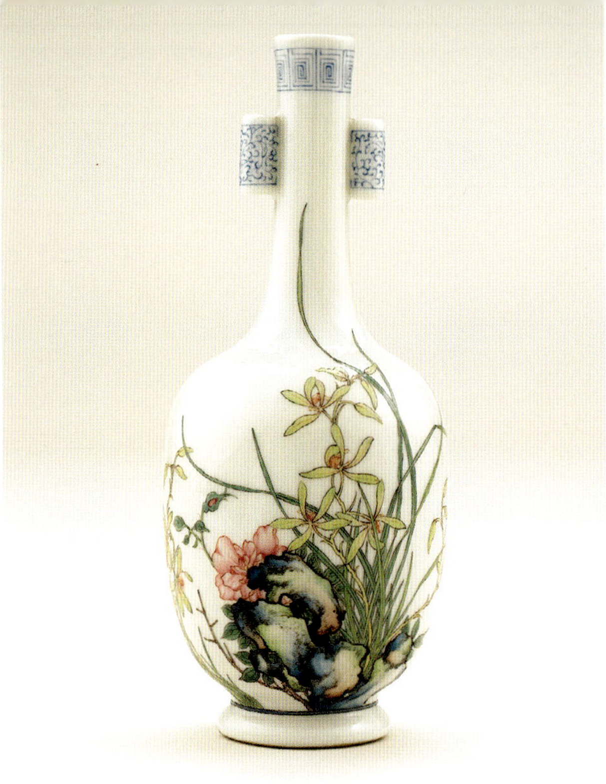

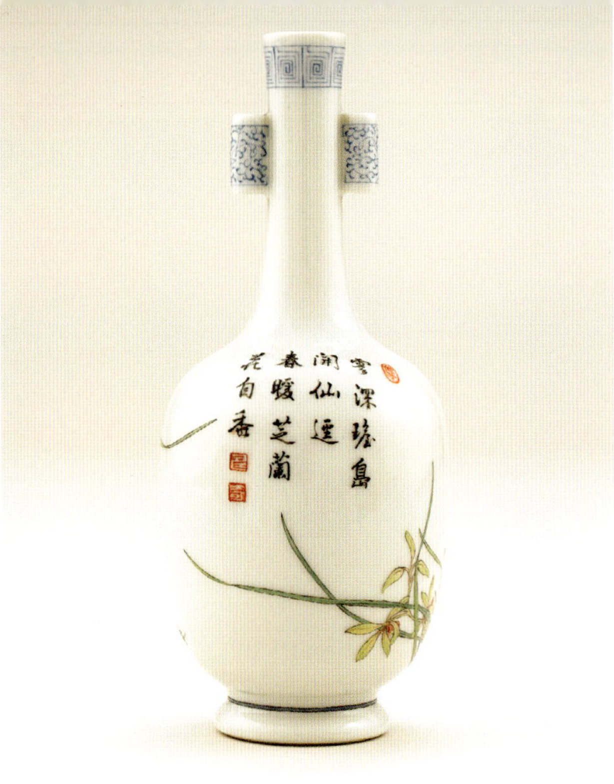

49 Vase painted with orchids and *lingzhi*
Porcelain made in Jingdezhen, Jiangxi province; decoration added in Beijing
素瓷器：江西景德鎮燒製；北京加琺瑯彩
Qing dynasty, Qianlong mark and period, AD 1736–95
Height 14.9 cm
PDF 829

The Qianlong emperor was a great collector of antiques and patron of the arts. He also appreciated the latest in modern technology. This porcelain vase combines these three great passions. It is modelled on the shape of an antique 'arrow pot', a vessel with short tubes either side of the narrow neck. People played a drinking game of pitching arrows into larger bronze and ceramic pots of this shape. Furthermore the enamel decoration demonstrates the extraordinary skill of porcelain decorators who worked within the palace. The painting of orchids and 靈芝, *lingzhi* [longevity fungus] with rocks is complemented by a fourteen-character poem:

> 雲深瓊島開仙逕，春暖芝蘭花自香, *yun shen qiong dao kai xian jing; chun ruan zhi lan hua zi xiang*
> A small path opens for the immortals through the deep clouds to paradise island; in the warm spring fragrance comes from iris and orchid flowers.

The three seals read 郁心, *yuxin* [elegant heart], 壽, *shou* [longevity] and 奇, *qi* [marvellous]. The four-character Qianlong *nianzhi* reign mark is written in standard script in blue enamel on the base.

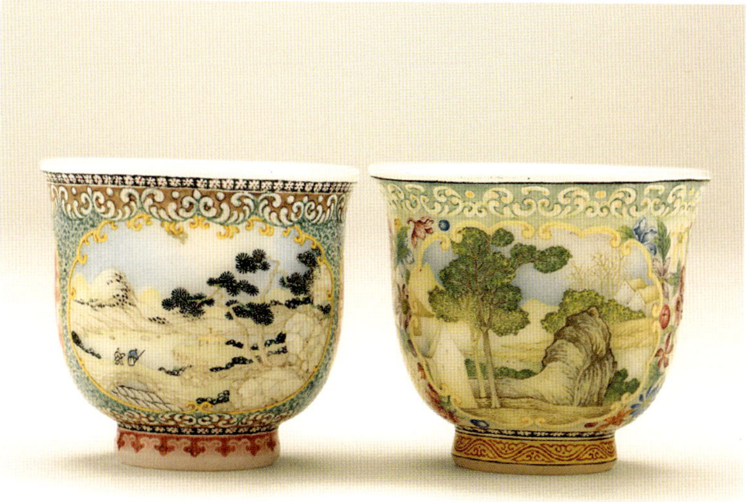

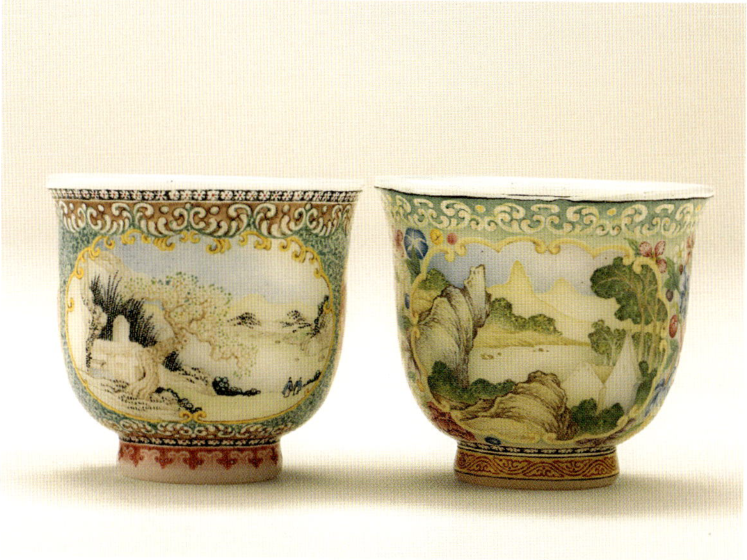

50 Two enamelled glass wine cups
Beijing 北京
Qing dynasty, Qianlong mark and period, AD 1736–95
Heights 4.6 cm, 4.5 cm
PDF 850 and 851

Enamelled glass painted within the same workshops as porcelain in the Forbidden City is much rarer than enamelled porcelain. Chinese glassmaking technology has traditionally been influenced by foreign craftsmen and the palace workshops were supervised by European Jesuits. Although these opaque white glass cups derive their shape from contemporary Qing porcelain made at Jingdezhen, the enamel decoration is informed by European painting styles. The landscape scenes of the cup on the right are depicted using Western perspective with receding sight lines. The companion cup has small panels in rose enamels between the landscape scenes that are both populated by two tiny Chinese figures. The border fill is decorated with tiny flowers in a technique popular with Venetian glassmakers. These cups have four-character Qianlong reign marks in blue enamel on their bases.

Selected Marks and Bases

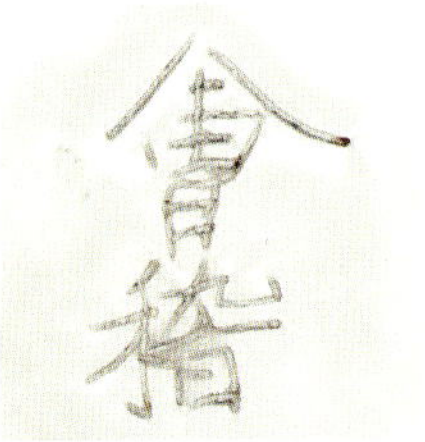

No. 2 (PDF 173)

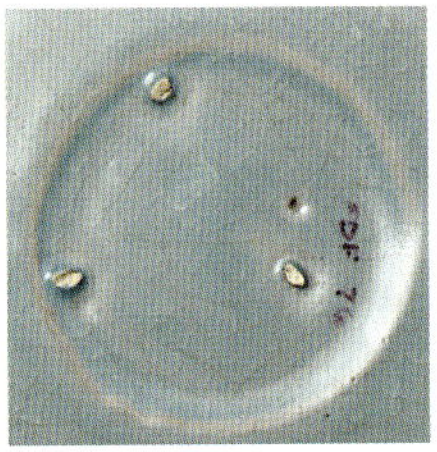
No. 4 (PDF 76)

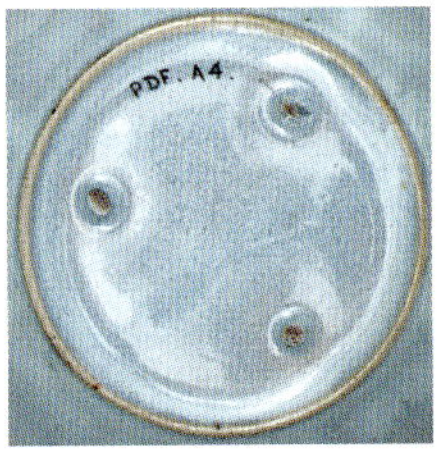
No. 10 (PDF A4)

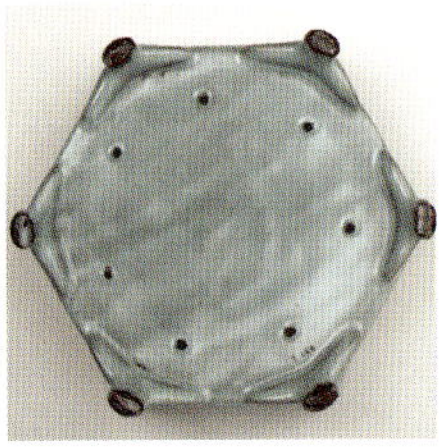
No. 15 (PDF 6)

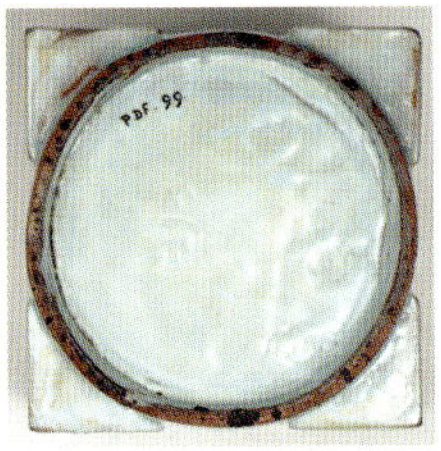
No. 16 (PDF 99)

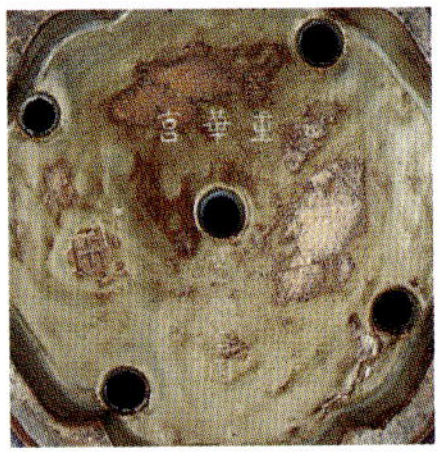
No. 21 (PDF A11)

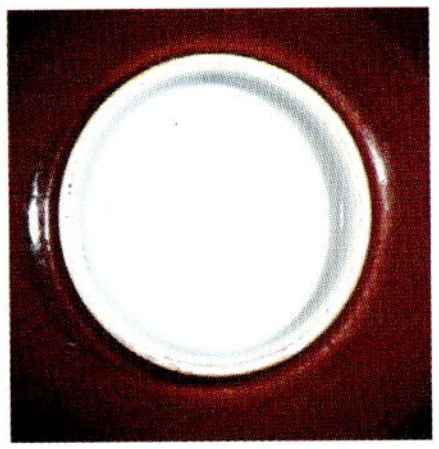
No. 32 (PDF 585)

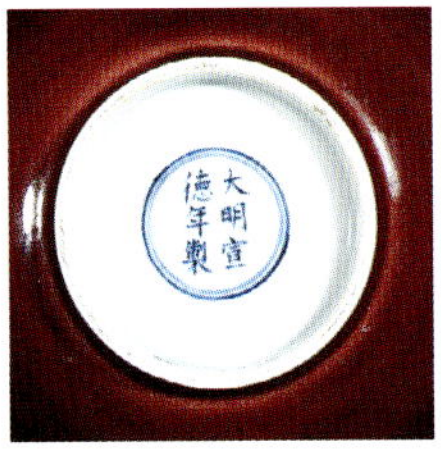

No. 32 (PDF A529)

No. 36 (PDF A644)

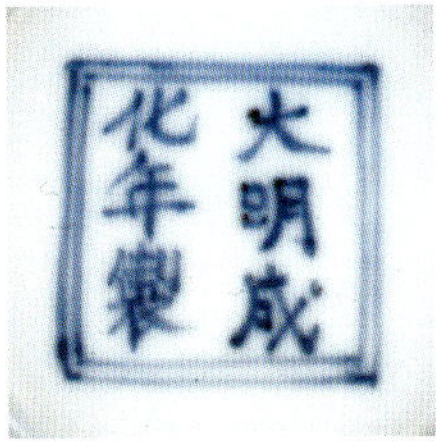

No. 36 (PDF B681)

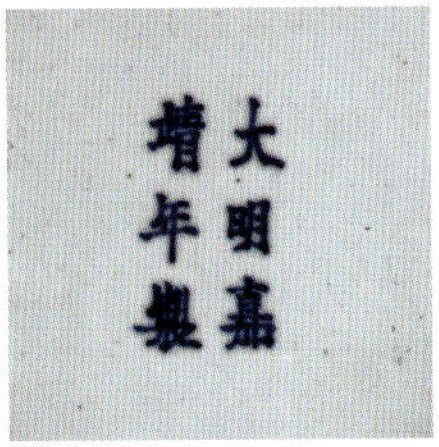

No. 39 (B617)

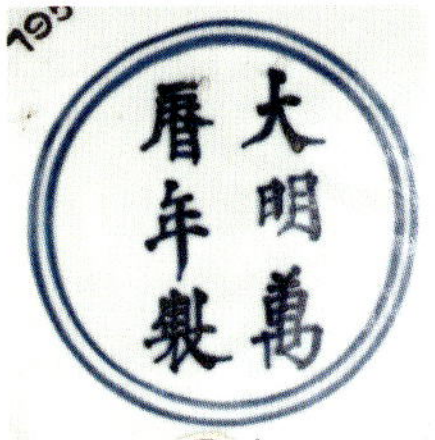

No. 40 (PDF 795)

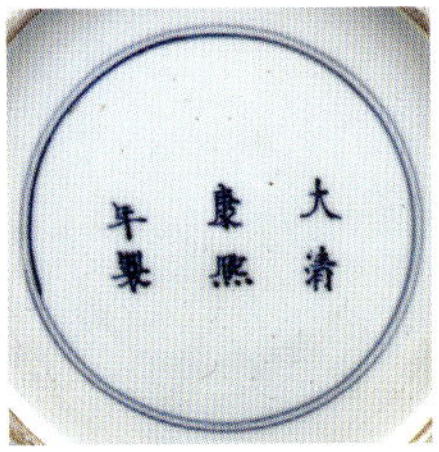

No. 41 (PDF C644)

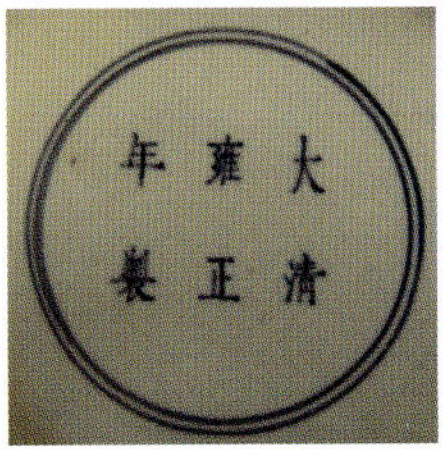

No. 42 (PDF 823)

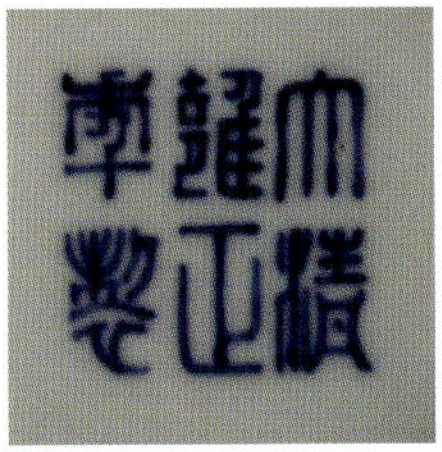
No. 43 (PDF A798)

No. 45 (PDF A806)

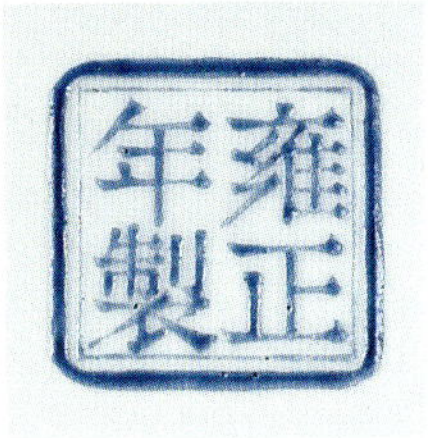

No. 46 (PDF A808)

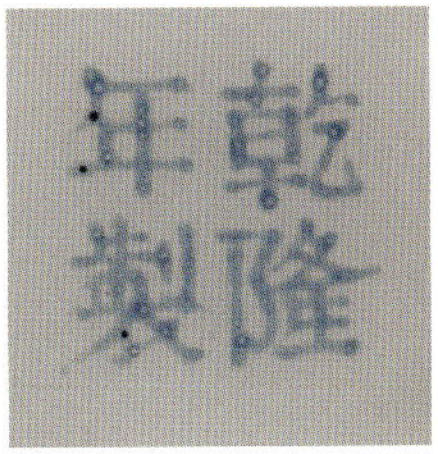

No. 50 (PDF 851)

Fig. 9 (PDF 836)

Fig. 10 (PDF A818)

Selected Bibliography

Chenghua ciqi tezhan/Special Exhibition of Ch'eng-hua Porcelain Ware, 1465–1487, exhibition catalogue, National Palace Museum, Taipei, 2003

Da guan: Bei Song Ruyao tezhan/Grand View: Special exhibition of Ju ware from the Northern Sung dynasty, National Palace Museum, Taipei, 2006

Lady David, 'Introduction' in Rosemary E. Scott, *Percival David Foundation of Chinese Art*, London, 1989, pp. 9–26

Ding yao bai ci tezhan tulu/Catalogue of the Special Exhibition of Ting Ware White Porcelain, exhibition catalogue, National Palace Museum, Taipei, 1987

Du Zhengxian (ed.), *Hangzhou Laohudong yaozhi ciqi jingxuan* [Selection of porcelains from the Laohudong kiln sites in Hangzhou], Beijing, 2002

Geng Baochang, *Ming Qing ciqi jianding* [Appraisal of Ming and Qing porcelain], Hong Kong, 1993

Geng Baochang (ed.), *Gugong Bowuyuan cang Ming chu qinghua ci* [Early Ming blue-and-white porcelain in the Palace Museum], 2 vols, Beijing, 2002

Geng Baochang (ed.), *Gugong Bowuyuan cang Qingdai yuyao ciqi* [Porcelains from the Qing dynasty imperial kilns in the Palace Museum collection], vol. 1, parts 1 and 2, Beijing, 2005

Jessica Harrison-Hall, *Catalogue of Late Yuan and Ming Ceramics in the British Museum*, London, 2001

R.L. Hobson, *A Catalogue of Chinese Pottery and Porcelain in the Collection of Sir Percival David Bt FSA*, London, 1934

Imperial Porcelain: Recent Discoveries of Jingdezhen Ware, exhibition catalogue, Museum of Oriental Ceramics, Osaka, 1995

Jingdezhen Zhushan chutu Yongle guanyao ciqi [Yongle imperial porcelain excavated at Zhushan, Jingdezhen], exhibition catalogue, Capital Museum, Beijing, 2007

Kangxi, Yongzheng, Qianlong: Qing porcelain from the Palace Museum Collection, Hong Kong, 1989

Rose Kerr, *Chinese Ceramics: Porcelain of the Qing dynasty 1644–1911*, London, 1986

Rose Kerr, *Song Dynasty Ceramics*, London, 2004

Rose Kerr and Nigel Wood, *Science and Civilisation in China*, vol. 5: *Chemistry and Chemical Technology*, part XII: *Ceramic Technology*, Cambridge, 2004

Regina Krahl, *Chinese Ceramics in the Topkapi Saray Museum, Istanbul*, ed. John Ayers, 3 vols, London, 1986

Peter Y. K. Lam, 'The David Vases Revisited: Annotation Notes of the Dedicatory Inscriptions', *Orientations,* November–December 2009, pp. 70–77

Li Baoping, 'Numbered Jun Wares: Controversies and new kiln site discoveries', *Transactions of the Oriental Ceramic Society*, vol. 71, London, 2008, pp. 65–77

Lin Shimin, *Qingci yu Yueyao/Celadon and Yue Kilns*, Shanghai, 1999

Mingdai Xuande guanyao jinghua tezhan tulu/Catalogue of the Special Exhibition of Selected Hsüan-te Imperial Porcelains of the Ming Dynasty, exhibition catalogue, National Palace Museum, Taipei, 1998

Hugh Moss, *By Imperial Command: An introduction to Ch'ing imperial painted enamels*, Hong Kong, 1976

Stacey Pierson, *Collectors, Collections and Museums: The field of Chinese ceramics in Britain, 1560–1960*, Bern, 2007

Stacey Pierson, *Earth, Fire and Water: Chinese ceramic technology: A handbook for non-specialists*, London, 1996

Rosemary Scott (ed.), *Chinese Copper Red Wares*, Percival David Foundation Monograph Series no. 3, School of Oriental and African Studies, University of London, London, 1992

Shanghai Bowuguan cang Kangxi ci tulu/Kangxi Porcelain Wares from the Shanghai Museum Collection, Hong Kong, 1998

Songdai Yaozhou yaozhi [Yaozhou kiln sites of the Song dynasty], Beijing, 1998

Song guanyao tezhan/Catalogue of the Special Exhibition of Sung Dynasty Kuan Ware, exhibition catalogue, National Palace Museum, Taipei, 1989

Treasures from the Underground Palaces: Excavated treasures from Northern Song pagodas, Dingzhou, Hebei province, China, exhibition catalogue, Idemitsu Museum of Arts, Tokyo, 1997

Ts'ai Ho-pi, *Qing gongzhong falangcai ci tezhan/Special Exhibition of Ch'ing Dynasty Enamelled Porcelains of the Imperial Ateliers*, exhibition catalogue, National Palace Museum, Taipei, 1992

Shelagh Vainker, *Chinese Pottery and Porcelain*, London, 2006

Wang Qingzheng, Fan Dongqing and Zhou Lili, *Ruyao de faxian/The Discovery of Ru Kiln*, Shanghai, 1987, rev. English edn, Hong Kong, 1991

Wang Qingzheng, *Yue yao, Mise ci/Yue Ware, Miseci Porcelain*, Shanghai, 1996

Nigel Wood, *Chinese Glazes: Their origins, chemistry and recreation*, London, 1999

Xie Chunlong (ed.), *Shanglinhu Yue yao* [Yue kilns at Shanglinhu], Beijing, 2002

Ye Peilan, *Yuandai ciqi* [Porcelain of the Yuan dynasty], Beijing, 1998

Ye Peilan (ed.), *Qing Porcelain of Kangxi, Yongzheng and Qianlong Periods from the Palace Museum Collection*, Hong Kong, 1989

Yuan and Ming Blue and White Ware from Jiangxi, Jiangxi Provincial Museum and Art Museum, The Chinese University of Hong Kong, Hong Kong, 2002

Zhu Boqian, *Longquan yao qingci/Celadons from Longquan Kilns*, Taipei, 1998

Index of Chinese Names and Terms